NEEDLECRAFTS

NEEDLECRAFTS

50 Extraordinary Gifts and Projects, Step by Step

Gillian Souter

CROWN TRADE PAPERBACKS

New York

Published by Crown Trade Paperbacks, 201 East 50th Street, New York, New York 10022. Member of the Crown Publishing Group.

Random House, Inc. New York, Toronto, London, Sydney, Auckland

CROWN TRADE PAPBERBACKS and colophon are trademarks of Crown Publishers, Inc.

Originally published in Australia by Off the Shelf Publishing in 1997.

Printed in Hong Kong

LIBRARY OF CONGRESS CATALOGING-IN-PUBLICATION DATA
is available upon request.

ISBN 0-609-80034-5

10 9 8 7 6 5 4 3 2 1

First American Edition

Foreword

Like many people, I was lucky to have a grandmother who was a prodigious stitcher – needlepoint, knitting, crochet, embroidery – she was skilled at them all. As a child, I inevitably failed to give any of these arts the attention they deserved but in recent years they have caught my imagination. While there may be less time available now for fine and detailed needlework, the pleasure to be gained by sitting still and concentrating on a piece of embroidery can be immense. This book may encourage you to take the time to revisit some of these traditional needlecrafts and to consider their potential for brightening our lives.

In addition to the well established crafts, this book touches on more modern techniques, such as machine embroidery, and includes chapters on making tassels and cords, which are invaluable as trims for needlecraft projects. Each chapter is accompanied by three sample projects:

A personal item, ideal as a gift

Something useful for the home

A memento to mark a special occasion

Items which have been lovingly stitched are ideal as presents and so this book concludes with a few ideas for wrapping gifts and making greeting cards. Knowing how I still treasure my grandmother's needlework, I can promise that your efforts with the needle will be much appreciated.

Contents

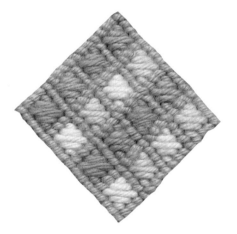

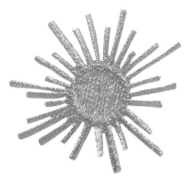

Yarns

What holds this book together is not, as the title might suggest, a needle. Rather, the common thread is just that: thread.

Threads or yarns are twisted fibers – cotton, wool, nylon, etc – which can be used for stitching, knitting or weaving. Thread tends to refer to finer lengths, yarn is reserved for heavier or coarser types.

There are general rules, formed over centuries, which dictate that wool should be used for needlepoint, stranded cotton for cross-stitch and so on, but such rules can be broken. There are so many types of yarn available, and new ones frequently appearing, that there is good reason for experimentation.

Your choice of yarn should really be determined by several things: the project's function, the nature of the other materials being used, and the stitches you plan to work. (Of course, you may have found a wonderful yarn and want to plan a project around it, but this is less likely.) You should consider whether the project will need to be laundered frequently or whether it will be framed. Will the yarn distort the fabric too much? Will it cover the canvas? Do you want stitches to have a matte finish or a sheen? Are the stitches intended to be delicate or dramatic?

There are several companies which produce yarns and sell them worldwide. Where specific colors are required for projects in this book, the number has been given for the DMC color, but you can select from other brand ranges if you prefer.

Threads can be bought from needlework stores and from many large department stores. Some companies also run mail order services; their addresses can be found in advertisements in needlework magazines.

Sewing threads are necessary for many of the projects. Special sewing threads are available for quilting and for machine embroidery.

Stranded cotton or floss is one of the most popular and versatile yarns. It can be divided or used whole.

Soft embroidery cotton has a matte finish and is 5-ply, so should be used on heavier fabrics or fine canvas.

Shaded or gradated yarns are available in different forms and can add interest to plain stitchwork.

Perlé thread is a very lustrous 2-ply thread, available in varying thicknesses.

Some cotton yarns are produced specifically for working delicate crochet projects. The thicker ones are also suitable for candlewicking embroidery.

Metallic threads are more readily available now than ever before and are available in colors, as well as gold and silver.

The most popular wool yarns for embroidery and needlepoint are crewel wool (2-ply) and tapestry wool (4-ply). For crochet and knitting, heavier wools are often used.

Equipment

The most important piece of equipment for a needleworker is a pair of steady hands. Treat them well: remember to take a break regularly from needlework that is repetitive or awkward to hold. The needlecraft workbox can be a relatively simple affair, although there are numerous products that we are encouraged to buy as patchworkers, quilters, cross-stitchers, and so on.

A selection of needles is essential. The two main types are sharp needles, such as crewel needles which have long eyes and are suitable for fine and medium embroidery, and what I've called blunt needles, which have a rounded end less prone to piercing the threads of the fabric. The latter are often called tapestry needles, but they can also be used for cross-stitch, for darning in knitting ends, and for other forms of needlework.

Equipment and materials for each project are listed in a box above the main picture. When the list includes 'sewing equipment' you will need a suitable needle, pins, sewing thread, a pair of scissors and a tape measure.

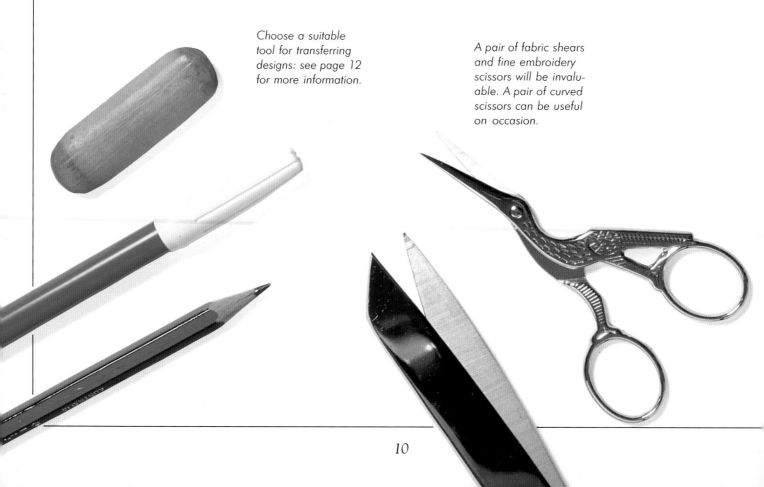

Choose a suitable tool for transferring designs: see page 12 for more information.

A pair of fabric shears and fine embroidery scissors will be invaluable. A pair of curved scissors can be useful on occasion.

An unpicking device and a thimble will be useful for some projects.

Most of the sewing work in this book can be done by hand, but a machine will speed up the more tedious aspects and can also be used for innovative embroidery.

The size of the eye, the shape of the tip, and the length all need to be considered when selecting a needle.

In most cases, using an embroidery hoop is a matter of preference. In certain cases, a hoop or frame is recommended.

Basic Techniques

The start and finish of needlecraft projects are often the most difficult parts and so some tips on these aspects follow. In between, you may be required to draw on very simple sewing techniques such as basting, or sewing hems and seams. If these terms are unfamil-iar, ask a friend to demonstrate the techniques, or refer to a book on basic sewing.

Before starting a project, it may help to read the opening pages of that chapter. Instructions for various embroidery stitches can be found on page 123.

Transferring Designs

There are various ways of transferring patterns onto fabric; your choice depends on the tools available, the fabric's texture and color and the way the design will be worked. With the exception of counted work, in which a design is transferred from a chart, all methods require a tracing.

If the fabric is thin, you can tape the traced pattern onto a window or other light source and trace over it with a dissolvable marker, tailor's chalk, or a soft lead pencil. Tailor's chalk tends to be more visible on dark fabrics. Pencil cannot easily be removed and should only be used where the design will be covered with stitches.

Another method is to turn over the tracing, place it on the fabric and rework the pencil lines, producing a reversed image. Carbon paper, placed between tracing and fabric, produces an image that is not reversed.

A design traced onto tissue paper can be basted onto dark or difficult fabrics such as velvet; the paper is then torn away, leaving the stitches to mark the design.

◀ *Most patterns given in this book are full-size but some need to be enlarged. If you don't have access to a photocopier, square up as follows. Trace the pattern and rule a grid over it. To enlarge by 200%, rule a grid twice the size on fresh tracing paper and copy the pattern, square by square.*

Finishing

Projects may need a gentle wash on completion. If you've used washable fabric and color-fast cotton threads, embroidery can be handwashed in warm water using mild soap and without rubbing. Rinse well and roll the work in a clean towel, before hanging it to dry, away from direct sunlight. Lay the work face down on a towel and iron it gently. Silk threads or ribbons should be dry cleaned.

Knitting, crochet work, and needlepoint may all need to be blocked into shape: see the instructions below for this.

If needlework is not in regular use, store it between sheets of acid-free tissue paper.

▶ If finished needlepoint is distorted, it should be blocked back into shape. Pin the work on a piece of cardboard or polystyrene so that it is square. Spray it with water and leave it to dry.

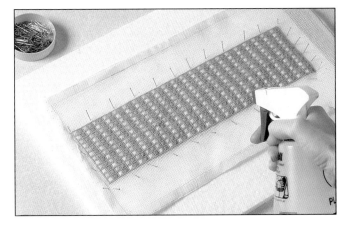

▶ To block knitting and crochet, gently handwash the work, following the instructions on the yarn label. Rinse well, and roll in a clean towel to remove excess water. Lay the work face up on dry, folded towels and use your hands to press it out to the desired shape. Secure the edges with rustproof pins. Allow the work to dry before removing it.

▶ To frame needlework, cut cardboard to fit your frame. Position the work over the cardboard and secure it temporarily with tape. Using strong thread and a needle, lace the edges of the fabric at the back, working top to bottom and then side to side (or around for a circular frame). Fit in frame.

Braids & Cords

While cords and braids are not strictly a form of needlecraft, they play an important role in many needlecraft projects, particularly in the finishing of them. Cords are decorative ropes made from several strands twisted or woven together, sometimes with a core of other, less expensive, material. Braids, on the other hand, are formed by weaving cords or lengths of yarn together. They tend to be flat and so the different strands are visible.

Before the invention of zips, cords were used to lace sections of garments and furnishings together. They were also looped and knotted to form fastenings known as 'froggings' which often adorned mid-European military uniforms as well as Chinese costumes.

You can buy a wide range of cords and braids, but making your own allows you to match materials and, of course, gives a project that individual touch. Choose or make ones suitable for your purpose. A soft, flexible cord is needed to create tighter coils, loops and knots. Laces, ties, and drawstrings need to be smooth so they can run freely.

The thickness of most cords makes them unsuitable for working in and out of fabric in embroidery stitches. However, they can be arranged on fabric and couched down with small stitches in a fine thread. Project 50, near the back of the book, is an example.

Cord endings always need to be secured so they do not fray. Bind the cord with thread in a matching color and secure it by stitching through the core several times, then trim off the unwanted end.

The loose ends of cords need particular attention. A tight knot is one solution; adding a tassel-like fringe softens the knot. An alternative is to seal the end in white glue and cover it with a fitting which can be crimped tight.

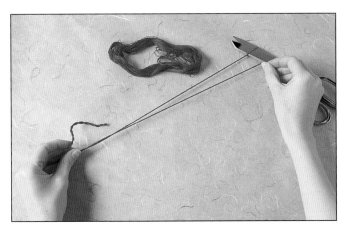

To twist one-color cord: cut several lengths of yarn, each approximately four times the length of the desired cord. Knot one end of the yarns to something stable and twist the other end. Holding the ends firmly, fold the cord in half and allow it to twist, a section at a time.

To twist two-color cord: in each color, cut several lengths of yarn, each approximately two times the length of the desired cord. Join the colors together at one end with an overhand knot. Secure one end of the joined threads to something stable and twist the other end. Holding the ends firmly, fold the cords in half at the color join and allow the colors to twist together, a section at a time.

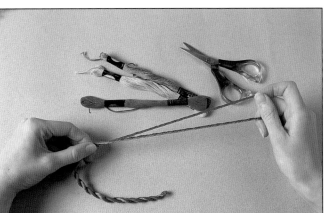

Carrick bend
This seemingly endless knot makes an attractive ornament. Small ones (with a loop added) can be used as closing devices on clothing. The large gold one is a double knot, made by weaving the cord a second time around, parallel to the first strand.

A core of doubled rope can be bound with stranded cotton in a figure-8 motion to make a decorative cord. The use of shaded or gradated threads adds extra interest.

PROJECT 1

Friendship Bands

YOU WILL NEED
embroidery cottons
scissors
a tape measure

Children love friendship bracelets in brightly colored cottons. They will also enjoy making them and giving them to best friends!

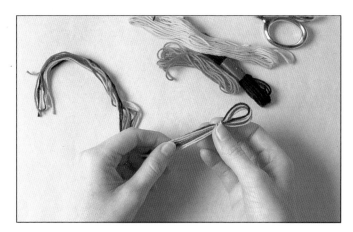

1 Cut five strands of soft embroidery cotton in different colors, each 30" long. Fold the bunch in half and make a knot at the top to form a loop as shown.

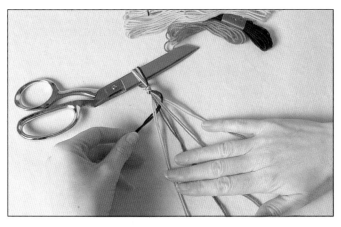

2 Secure the loop and spread out the strands in pairs. Weave the right-hand pair over the next pair, under the next pair, over the next pair and under the last pair. It should now be at the left.

3 Repeat step 2 over and over, always weaving the right-hand strands to the left. Continue until the braid is the desired length.

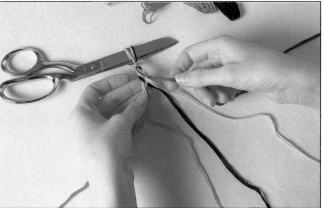

4 Secure the ends with an overhand knot. Snip open the loop at the other end and leave a fringe at each end for tying the band around the wrist. The more brightly colored band in the large picture is woven with three strands of each color, rather than two.

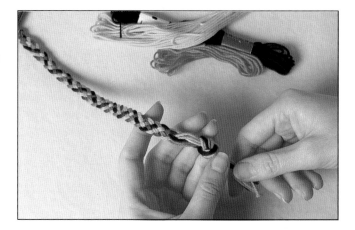

PROJECT 2

Lampshade

YOU WILL NEED
gold cord
black cord
a lampshade
strong tape
sewing equipment

Decorate a plain and inexpensive lampshade with Greek braid to create a stylish and individual piece for your home.

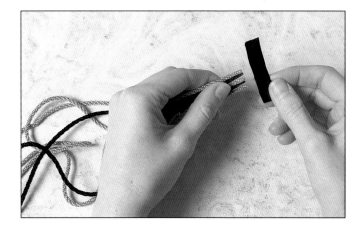

1 Cut two foundation cords slightly longer than the perimeter of your lampshade. Cut three braiding cords, each three times the length of the perimeter. Tape the ends together in the sequence shown.

2 Secure the taped end to a work surface. Pass the braiding cord on the far left over the next two cords. Pass the foundation cord at the left over the next braiding cord and pull it straight. Repeat these two actions, this time working on the right-hand side.

3 Continue as above, changing sides each time. Pull the foundation cords occasionally to straighten the braid. When the braid is the correct length, make sure it is neat and even. Bind the ends with more tape and trim them.

4 Sew the braid onto the lamp shade with strong thread and a large needle. Weave gold cord into a carrick bend (see page 15). Stitch this onto the shade to cover the joined braid ends.

PROJECT 3

Napkin Rings

These twisted cords in rich red, green and gold yarns will add a festive touch to your table around Christmas time.

1 ▶ Cut five lengths of red stranded cotton and five of green, each 39 " long. Fold these in half and link them as shown. Tie an overhand knot at each end of the looped threads.

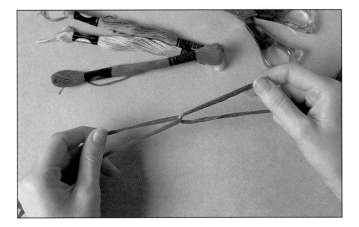

2 ▶ Secure one end of the looped threads to something stable and twist the other end. Holding the cord ends firmly, fold it in half at the color join and allow the colors to twist together, a section at a time.

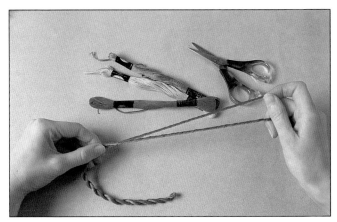

3 ▶ Arrange the cord into a double coil and test that it fits a rolled napkin. Bind the loose ends with stranded cotton and use a needle to bind this tightly to the folded end. Trim the ends neatly.

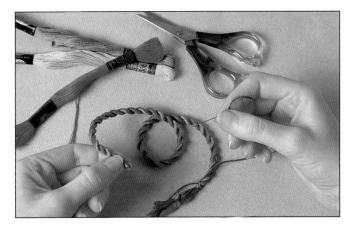

4 ▶ Make two tassels (see page 23 for instructions) using a 2 " piece of card. Do not cut the loops of the tassels. Braid the hanging threads and use this to tie the tassels onto the cord rings.

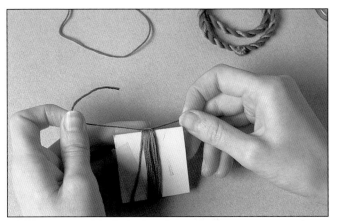

Tassels

Tassels may seem to be the invention of a frivolous mind, but they are the natural result of a frayed end of a cord, a common means of fastening garments and furnishings. The craft of making tassels and trimmings became an art form in France in the seventeenth century where it was known as *passementerie*.

Tassels add color and richness to furnishings and can look very stylish on the corners of cushions, as curtain tie-backs, or simply hanging from door knobs. They can also add interest to smaller items, such as wedding bouquets or evening bags, where their sheen and movement draws the eye.

Almost any yarn may be used to make a tassel: twine or raffia gives a natural effect, while gold thread makes a much more lavish statement. Long tassels should be made from fibers that hang well, such as silk or rayon cord. Experiment by mixing colors and textures for added contrast.

It is a good idea to make a note of measurements and yarn amounts as you work, as varying the weight of yarn or the thickness of the tassel will produce quite different results. Be generous with the tassel's skirt or body, determined by the number of times you wind the yarn around the cardboard pattern, or the tassel will look insipid. On the other hand, a tassel should not be too heavy for the fabric onto which it is sewn.

While the basic tassel is very easy to make, more complex and elaborate tassels require some planning and skill. Extra decoration can be added to the head of the tassel, or a number of tassels can be clustered together.

Rayon yarn is ideal for making long tassels and can be colored with cold-water dyes. For shorter tassels, stranded cotton can be used.

Tassels can, of course, adorn projects made from materials other than fabric, such as this marbled paper bookmark.

The different parts of a tassel are the skirt, neck, binding thread, head, hanging thread. In this example, the hanging thread is concealed in the bookmark.

▲ To make a basic tassel, cut a piece of cardboard to the desired height of the tassel. Lay a short piece of yarn across the card. Wind a length of yarn around the card until it is the desired thickness. Tie the short yarn so the loops are tightly gathered; the ends now form the hanging threads. Slip the loops off the card and bind

the neck with another piece of yarn, concealing the ends in the body of the tassel. Trim the base of the loops.

A simple tassel can also be hooded with buttonhole stitching, as in Project 5.

The head of the tassel below has been covered with cord woven in a Turks's head knot.

The beautiful multiple tassel is made with a wooden former on to which many small tassels are attached. A frilled braid covers the neck.

PROJECT 4

Scissors Tassel

YOU WILL NEED
embroidery yarn
gold thread
scissors
card
a tape measure

This elegant decoration for your needlework scissors draws on techniques for making both cords as well as tassels.

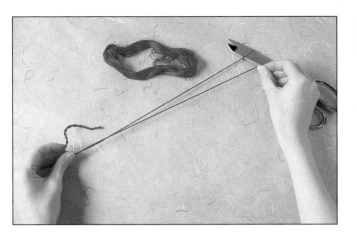

1 Cut six 1 yard lengths of embroidery yarn (coton à broder has been used here). Make a twisted cord, as shown on page 15. Bind the ends of the cord together with matching thread to form a loop.

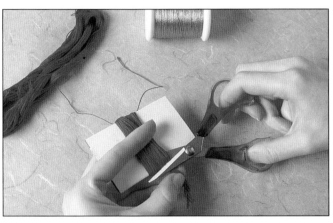

2 Make a basic tassel using a 2 " card, by following the instructions on page 23. Bind the neck of the tassel with gold thread.

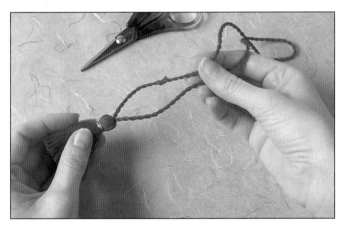

3 Use the tassel's hanging threads to attach it to the cord, then conceal the ends back in the tassel. Tie an overhand knot a short distance above the tassel, concealing the bound cord ends.

4 Loop the cord through one of the fingerholes on the scissors and thread the tassel through the loop to tie a lark's head knot.

PROJECT 5

Cushions

A plain cushion can be given lots of extra style with such trimmings as these hooded tassels and a laced binding.

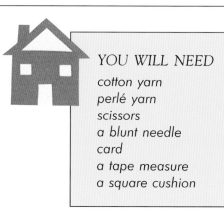

YOU WILL NEED
cotton yarn
perlé yarn
scissors
a blunt needle
card
a tape measure
a square cushion

1 ▶ *Make four basic tassels using a 3½" card, by following the instructions on page 23. Bind the neck of each tassel with one end of a 6½' length of perlé yarn.*

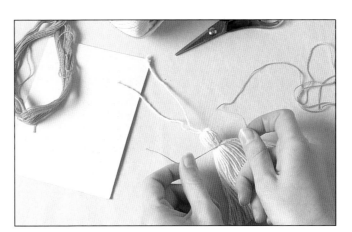

2 ◀ *Thread the other end of the perlé yarn through a blunt needle. Hold the head of the tassel towards you and work large, evenly spaced buttonhole stitches around the neck. When you reach the first stitch, start a second row of stitches, and so on.*

3 ▶ *Continue spiraling up around the tassel head, tightening the stitches as you reach the top. Knot the yarn onto the tassel's hanging thread and conceal the end in the body of the tassel.*

4 ◀ *Use each tassel's hanging threads to sew it onto the cushion corner, knotting the threads securely inside the cushion. With another length of perlé yarn, whip around the piping twice to create a laced effect.*

PROJECT 6

Key Tassel

Tassels can be as elaborate as you like. This one, made with yarn which has been hand-dyed, would make an unusual gift.

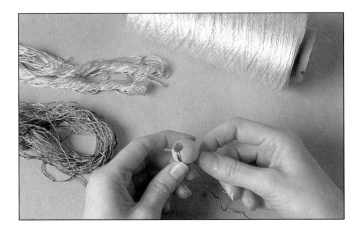

1 Dye hanks of rayon yarn with cold water dyes, or buy colored yarns. Cover a large wooden bead with yarn by threading it through the hole. Knot the ends when finished.

2 Make a large tassel using a 3 " card, by following the instructions on page 23. This will be the core tassel and should be very thick.

3 Cut 30 " yarn in the first color and a matching piece in the second color. Knot them together at one end and make a twisted cord (see page 15). Knot the ends to secure and make four more cords in this way.

4 In the second color, make five outer tassels using a 3 " card. These should each be approximately one-fifth the thickness of the core tassel. Use the twisted cords from step 3 as the hanging threads and bind the necks of these outer tassels in the contrasting color.

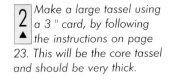

5 Assemble the tassel by threading all the hanging threads through the hole in the bead. Tie an overhand knot above the bead so the tassels are secured below. Thread the other ends through the hole in a key and knot them tightly. Trim the tassels evenly.

Beadwork

For thousands of years beads have been used for making exquisite jewelry and for embellishing clothing and furnishings. In earlier times when all beads were shaped by hand, only the wealthy could afford to buy them. Today their price, variety and availability means anyone who wishes to decorate with beads can do so. Many cities have specialist bead stores which are a veritable Aladdin's cave, and beads are also sold by mail order in many countries.

Beads come in all shapes and sizes. Most are drilled through the center but drop beads are drilled through the top and serve as a good end bead in a fringe. Glass and plastic beads can be washed with a garment. When planning a beaded project consider the number of beads you will require and their total weight.

Embroidered beads can add sparkle to plain fabrics or can be used to highlight a printed design. A border decoration of beads gives a finished appearance to an item. Sketch your rough design onto scrap paper before transferring it onto fabric. If the design is too complex to be marked on fabric with tailor's chalk, copy it onto tissue paper. Stitch the tissue onto the fabric, tearing it away once the design is marked with basting lines or when the beads are sewn in place.

Complex beading should be worked on the fabric before it is made up. If the fabric is thin, line it with a heavier material before beading. Use a strong thread, matching the fabric or beads as closely as possible. You will need a thin needle with a tiny eye to fit through the beads so a needle threader may come in handy.

Beads of a uniform size, such as seed beads, can also be woven together on a simple loom to create decorative strips or blocks of design. Project 9 is an example of this craft.

Strong thread or fine wire are required for stringing beads.

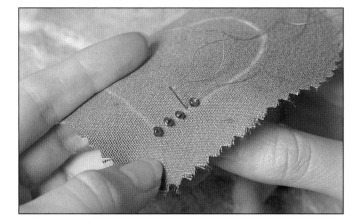

▲ Single beads, or those stitched widely apart, can be secured on fabric with back stitches. Secure the thread and bring the needle up to the front of the fabric. Thread a bead onto the needle and then make a bead-sized stitch back from right to left. Bring up the needle in front of the next bead's position.

Gold beads look stunning on either light or dark fabrics. Those on the decoration above are glass seed beads. The velvet bag below is worked with plastic beads in two shapes.

▲ To couch a string of beads, secure a double thread on the reverse of the fabric. Thread on a number of beads and position the string as desired. Secure another needle and thread near the starting point. Make a small stitch over the first thread, between the first and second bead.

Bring the needle up again at the next interval and continue, working along the beads.

PROJECT 7

Beaded Fringe

YOU WILL NEED
fabric
beads
strong thread
a beading needle
sewing equipment

A beautiful piece of fabric can be made even more special with the addition of a beaded fringe. Choose beads that aren't too heavy.

1 ▶ *Plan your arrangement of beads. The fringe shown uses a combination of seed and pebble beads. Turn, press and sew a hem in fabric that is at least medium weight.*

2 ▶ *Cut a length of strong polyester thread and thread it through a long needle with a small eye. Secure the thread at the back of the hem and bring it out at the bottom edge.*

3 ▶ *Pick up the selected beads and pass the needle through a small bead which acts as a stopper and will not reveal too much of the thread.*

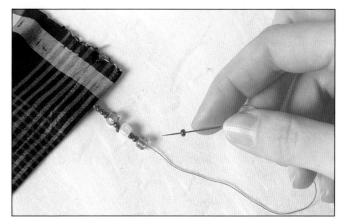

4 ▶ *Thread the needle back up through the other beads and through the fabric, securing it near the starting point at the back of the hem. On the next stitch, bring the needle out further along the hem and work the next strand of the fringe.*

PROJECT 8

Pearl Collar

This necklace can be made with glass pearls or even plastic ones. It would make a dramatic statement at a wedding or other special event.

YOU WILL NEED

$^1/_8$" *pearl beads*
$^3/_{16}$" *pearl beads*
beading thread
a beading needle
a clasp
crimps
pliers
scissors

1 ▶ *Cut 6 ' of white beading thread and thread it through a suitable needle. Thread on a crimp, then a clasp and knot tightly. Return back through the crimp and push it close to the clasp. Secure by squashing the crimp tight with pliers.*

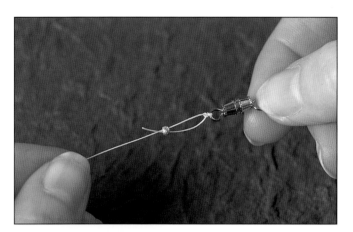

2 ◀ *Sort piles of ¹/₈ " beads (small) and ³/₁₆ " beads (large). Thread onto the needle the following beads: one large, one small, one large, one small, seven large.*

3 ▶ ** Thread the needle through the second small bead once again. Then thread on the following: one large, one small, one large, one small, one large bead. Thread the needle through the second last large bead on the previous loop.*

4 ◀ *Add five large beads. Repeat from * until the necklace is the desired length. Finish it off so the end matches the beginning. Thread the end through another crimp and the other half of the clasp, knot it, then back through the crimp and the last three beads. Squash the crimp securely and trim the thread.*

PROJECT 9

Comb Case

Bead weaving is a craft perfected by North American Indians. You will need an inexpensive bead loom, or you can improvise with an empty picture frame.

YOU WILL NEED
a bead loom
beading thread
a beading needle
seed beads
strong tape
felt or leather
sewing equipment

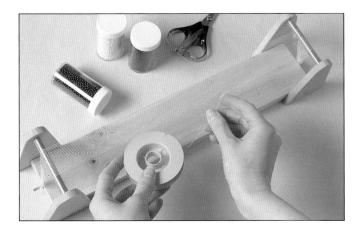

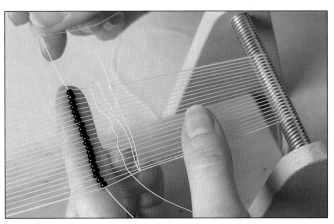

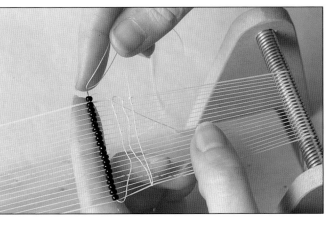

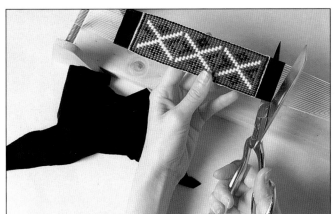

1 Thread the loom with warp threads as shown. For this project you will need 22 warp threads, but double the side threads for strength. Cut a long thread for the weft and knot it on one side of the warp.

2 Weave the weft thread through the warp threads twice. Load the beads for the first row onto the needle in the sequence shown on the pattern below. Push the beads onto the thread and, using your finger, press them up in place between the warp threads.

3 Hold the beads in place while you bring the needle back through the beads, this time over the warp threads. Now work the next row. Try to select beads of a uniform size, rejecting any that are extra large or small. If you need to join weft threads, try to conceal the knot in the beading.

4 When complete, weave the weft twice and tie off. Apply strong tape across the warp at either end and trim the excess threads. Cut two pieces of felt or leather just larger than the weaving. Fold the taped ends in and sew the weaving onto one piece, then sew the two pieces together around three sides to form a pocket.

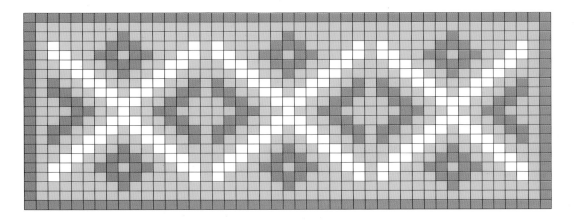

Ribbonwork

Traditionally, ribbons have been used for decoration, as status symbols, tokens of love, badges of allegiance. Nowadays, they are less expensive but still precious. Ribbons can be made of silk, satin, rayon, chiffon, or any number of fabrics. They are very versatile to work with: they can be woven, braided, embroidered, appliquéd or made into bows or roses. It is worthwhile having a collection of ribbons in different types, widths and colors, so you can always choose something to suit your current project.

Since the eighteenth century, ribbon embroidery has been used to adorn clothing and accessories and this form of decorative work is currently enjoying a resurgence of popularity. Embroidering with ribbons is like working with a broad brush when painting. The look that might be achieved with multiple stitches in traditional embroidery can perhaps be achieved with a single ribbon stitch which has both width and height. Silk ribbons are particularly beautiful to work with, although they are also fragile and fray easily.

Regular stitches, such as straight stitch, French knots and stem stitch can be used, but there are also some stitches that have been specially developed for ribbon embroidery, such as the loop stitch used in Project 10. If embroidering ribbon on garments, use closely stitched designs that won't unravel when washed. If your project is to be framed, you can use a larger, looser stitch. Take care that the ribbon does not twist when you are working with it. A blunt needle or toothpick can be useful to control stitches and to keep the ribbon straight.

Lock the ribbon on the needle by threading it, piercing it near one end and pulling the other end.

1 ◄ To make a ribbon rose, start by folding one end of the ribbon towards you to form a stem. Roll the stem along the ribbon until you have formed the center of the rose.

2 ► Fold the ribbon towards you but do not crease the fold. Roll the rose along the fold at an angle, so that the ribbon flares out to form a petal shape. When you reach the end of the fold, repeat this step. When the rose is the desired size, taper the ribbon down towards the stem. Secure the stem with several stitches. Trim the ends.

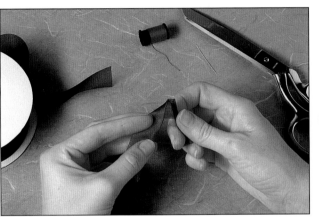

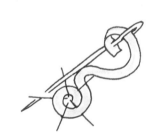

Spiderweb rose
Stitch five spokes with a strand of embroidery cotton. Bring the ribbon up near the center and weave it under and over the spokes, allowing the ribbon to twist as you work.

This pretty purse is decorated with French knots, straight stitch, and spiderweb roses all in ribbon, along with stem stitch and tiny beads.

PROJECT 10

Napkins

YOU WILL NEED
linen fabric
silk ribbons
stranded cotton
sewing equipment

Embroidering with silk ribbons can produce most realistic effects, especially when working floral designs such as these pansies.

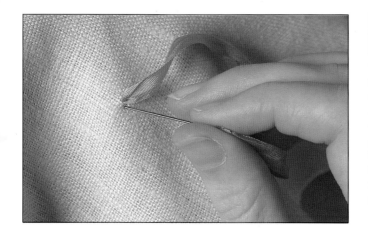

1 ◄ Cut a square of linen and hem all four sides. Thread a needle with an ³/₈ " purple ribbon. Bring it through the fabric near one corner and then back down a short distance away, forming a loop. Repeat this to form a petal from two parallel loops, then sew two more petals like this. Secure each loop to the fabric with tiny concealed stitches in sewing thread.

2 ► Thread a needle with ¹/₈ " yellow silk ribbon and make a straight stitch from the center of the flower into the center of a petal, pinning down the overlapping purple ribbons. Repeat this for each petal.

3 ► Thread a needle with a ¹/₈ " gold silk ribbon and work a French knot (see page 123) in the center of the flower.

4 ► Sew the leaf with a series of straight stitches in ¹/₈ " green silk ribbon, starting at the tip and working from side to side down to the stem. Backstitch the stem with 3 strands of green embroidery cotton.

PROJECT 11

Floss Tidy

YOU WILL NEED
satin ribbons
felt
interfacing
an iron
sewing equipment

Woven ribbons are used to make this charming roll for keeping your embroidery floss tidy while you work. You will need 9 yards of ⁵/₈" ribbon.

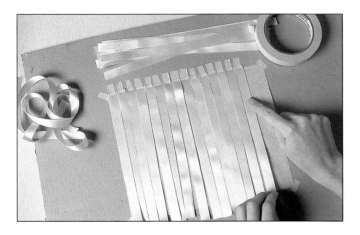

1 ▲ Cut an 11 x 9 " piece of iron-on interfacing and tape it, glue side up, on a work surface. Cut strips of $^5/_8$ " ribbon and tape them along the top of the interfacing so they run vertically.

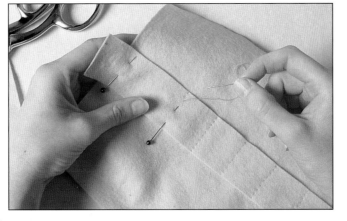

2 ▲ Weave strips of ribbon across the interfacing, taping them at either end as you work. When the weaving is complete, iron over it to fuse the ribbons onto the interfacing.

3 ▶ Cut a 10 x 8 " piece of felt. Cut a 10 x 1½ " strip of felt and lay it across the larger piece. Pin this at intervals and sew the two layers together to create loops for holding floss.

4 ▶ Trim the ribbon weaving to the same size as the felt. Lay the felt on the interfacing. Fold and pin a wide ribbon around the edges to bind all the layers. Stitch along the edges of the binding ribbon, piercing all the layers.

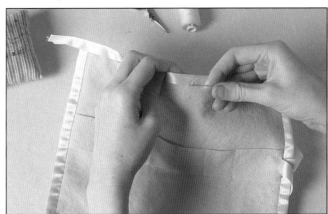

5 ▶ Fold a length of ribbon in half and secure it at one edge with a few stitches to form ties.

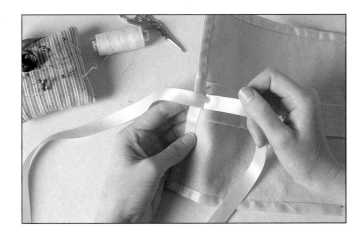

PROJECT 12

Floral Picture

This lavish bouquet of ribbon roses would make a delightful gift to mark a wedding anniversary or other romantic occasion.

YOU WILL NEED
backing fabric
silk ribbons
a hoop
sewing equipment
stiff cardboard
a compass
a knife
a cutting mat
a recessed frame

1 ◀ *Follow the steps on page 39 to roll a number of roses, using a soft, pliable ribbon.*

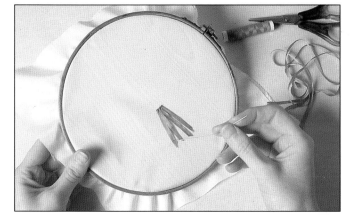

2 ▲ *Cut a piece of background fabric and place it in a hoop. Cut several lengths of narrow green ribbon and stitch them onto the fabric as stalks.*

3 ▲ *Stitch a length of ribbon into a loop. Cut another piece and wrap it around the loop to form a bow. Arrange the bow on the fabric and pin it in place, then secure it with small running stitches in a matching thread color.*

4 ▶ *Working from the center of the bow up, secure each rose in place with a couple of stitches in a matching thread color. Make sure the roses stand upright, so you can see into them.*

5 ▶ *Roll some half-formed roses to look like buds. Stitch these, lying flat, at the edge of the bunch. Make a few small stitches between them with green ribbon to suggest leaves. Cut a round piece of cardboard, lace the work over it and then frame it (see page 13 for instructions).*

Patchwork

Patchwork, also known as piecing, is the technique of sewing small pieces of fabric together to create a larger piece which can then be made into a quilt, a jacket, a wall hanging – indeed almost anything!

Traditionally, patches of fabric were worked in blocks. These are repeated units of shapes which, when stitched together, form the basis of the design as in Project 14. Simple repeat block patterns involving squares, rectangles or diamonds have the added advantage of economy in materials and space. The patterns possible with the block method are virtually unlimited. Individual blocks can be set apart by sashing: long strips of plain fabric. Juxtaposing blocks without sashing can create a secondary, more complex pattern. The piecing together of blocks can be done by hand, but a sewing machine speeds up the process greatly with no loss of quality. Paper patchwork (shown opposite) does, however, require hand sewing. The techique of using paper templates of uniform shape requires some precision and is ideal for smaller projects.

'Crazy' patchwork uses shapes which fit together in an irregular but economical way. Jig-saw like construction allows for the use of every available scrap of fabric, wasting none of what was once a valuable resource.

Cotton is the best fabric for patchwork; it's easy to handle and wears well. Today, many craft stores and mail order businesses sell small pieces of patterned cotton fabrics specifically for patchworkers. Although not really consistent with the craft's origins, this does give the designer a great range from which to select.

A rotary cutter, a clear grid ruler and a self-healing cutting mat are all worthwhile investments for anyone interested in patchwork.

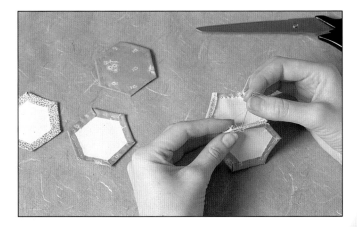

▲ *Paper-piecing is a time-consuming but highly accurate method of aligning patches. Papers, cut in the shape of the desired patch, are covered with fabric pieces and a seam is turned and basted. The patches are then stitched together with tiny overcasting stitches. Once the patchwork is complete, the basting is unpicked and the papers removed.*

Block patterns were very popular with early American settlers, for whom space and materials were limited. Blocks could be made individually and then assembled in a short space of time, often at a social gathering.

PROJECT 13

Shopping Bag

A bag like this is just what you need: it saves the planet from yet more paper and plastic bags, and adds a splash of color into the bargain!

YOU WILL NEED
cotton fabric scraps
strong lining fabric
interfacing
buttons
tape or ribbon
a measure
cutting equipment
a sewing machine
sewing equipment

1 Arrange fabric rectangles (with generous seam allowances around each piece) to form an irregular block with a wide band along the top. Sew the pieces together, pressing seams as you work, to create one side. Arrange and sew another side for the back. Fold and press a deep hem along the top band on each side.

2 Lay the two patchwork sections together, right sides facing, and sew a generous seam along the sides and base. Turn right side out. Cut two pieces of strong lining fabric the same dimensions as the patchwork. Fold and press a matching hem at the top and sew sides and base. Insert the lining bag into the patchwork bag.

3 For each handle, cut a strip of fabric 2½ times the desired handle width and extra long. For added strength, iron interfacing onto the wrong side. Lay tape or ribbon along the right side, fold the handle lengthwise, and seam the long edge and at one end. Turn the handle right side out, by pulling the tape. Press flat.

4 Insert each end of a handle between the outer and inner bags on one side, so that they extend past the top band of fabric. Sew handles firmly in place. Handsew the lining to the outer bag around the opening. Stitch a few buttons onto each side of the bag.

PROJECT 14

Country Mat

This rustic mat features a traditional block pattern known as 'Broken Dishes' in the center. There is a clever technique for piecing this design accurately and quickly.

YOU WILL NEED
cotton fabric scraps
lining fabric
wadding
bias binding
a ruler
a pencil
cutting equipment
a sewing machine
sewing equipment

1 Cut a 5⅝ " square of paper as a template. Use this to measure and cut two squares of fabric: one in fabric A and one in B. Lay one square on the other and draw an 'x' from corner to corner on the top square.

2 Machine sew ¼ " in from the drawn lines, as shown. With a rotary cutter, cut along the drawn lines. Open each of the four pieced triangles, press the seams, and set aside.

3 Use a 4½ " square paper template to cut four fabric squares: two in fabric A and two in fabric B. Repeat steps 1 and 2 with these to make eight pieced triangles. Join two of these to make a square as shown. Repeat with the six remaining triangles, making four squares in all. Press the seams.

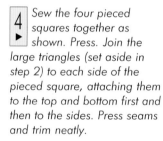

4 Sew the four pieced squares together as shown. Press. Join the large triangles (set aside in step 2) to each side of the pieced square, attaching them to the top and bottom first and then to the sides. Press seams and trim neatly.

5 Cut wadding and backing fabric the same size as the blocked piece and stack them with the blocked piece right side up. At each corner of the central square, make a single stitch in strong thread and knot the ends on the underside. Baste and then sew bias binding around the edges, securing all three layers.

PROJECT 15

Crazy Stocking

Scraps of rich fabric, arranged haphazardly and decorated with embroidery, imbue a gift stocking with all the excitement of Christmases past.

YOU WILL NEED
fabric scraps
lining fabric
embroidery threads
a pencil
paper
scissors
a sewing machine
sewing equipment

1 Enlarge the stocking pattern on page 158 by approximately 300% and use this as a template to mark and cut out two pieces of base fabric. From scraps of different fabric, cut random shapes and arrange them on one of the bases so that they overlap slightly. Pin in place.

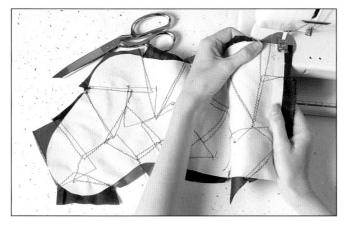

2 Machine sew the scraps onto the base, using a zigzag stitch in a dark thread. When all the scraps are secured, sew around the edge of the stocking shape. Trim the scraps and staystitch around the edges.

3 Embroider along the seams of each scrap, using two strands of embroidery thread and selecting from feather stitch, chain stitch and fly stitch (see page 123). Prepare the back of the stocking as above, making sure the scraps are sewn on the correct side of the base fabric.

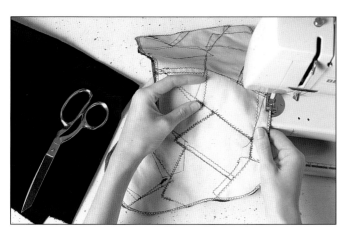

4 Lay the two sections together, right sides facing, and sew around the stocking, leaving the opening unsewn. Turn it right side out. Cut and sew a lining in dark fabric and insert it, wrong side out, into the stocking. Turn in the top edges and handsew the lining to the decorated stocking.

Appliqué

Appliqué is the technique of cutting out pieces of fabric and stitching them to a background, usually to create a pictorial or representational design. Originally developed as a means of extending the life of a garment or of making expensive materials go further, its esthetic appeal was quickly realized and exploited. Curved shapes can be more easily appliquéd than worked in pieced patchwork, and elaborate designs using motifs such as flowers, birds and fruit became a way of showing off the skills of a needlewoman.

Appliqué is often used in combination with quilting to produce bedspreads, but any project which shows off the appliqué to good effect is worth considering. Smaller projects might include cushions, table linen, or even the humble sweatshirt.

The method you choose for appliquéing should determine your choice of fabrics. If you plan to turn the edges of pieces under before stitching (which may be necessary if the project will require regular washing), fabrics from natural fibers – cotton, silk, wool – are best as they can be creased easily and folded at the edges. The backing fabric should be of similar weight to the appliqué.

Appliqué shapes can be basted into place on the base fabric with long running stitches, or attached with fusible webbing and a hot iron. The pieces can then be secured with slip-stitching or with decorative stitches such as buttonhole stitch. Alternatively, you can use a tight zigzag setting on a sewing machine to secure pieces with raw edges. With this method, you may need to use a commercial stabilizer to prevent the background fabric from puckering.

One of the properties of felt is that it doesn't fray. This makes it an ideal material for appliqué as there's no need to turn edges under before stitching shapes in place.

▲ Fusible webbing is a
paper-backed product
which can be cut to
shape and then used to fuse
appliqué pieces to the
backing fabric. You should
then secure the shapes with
stitches which will also
prevent fraying.

▲ In the traditional method,
a small seam allowance
is turned under before
appliqué pieces are sewn
onto backing fabric. To make
handling easier, the turned
seam can be basted first.

If you are working with lightweight
fabrics which do not hold a crease
well, or with very small shapes, you
may find it helpful to iron on interfacing
cut to shape. Alternatively, plastic-
coated freezer paper can be ironed
onto the back of appliqué shapes and
then removed before stitching onto
backing fabric is completed.

PROJECT 16

Kitchen Cover

YOU WILL NEED
felt
stranded cotton
tracing paper
a pencil
sewing equipment

Felt is a great material for appliqué as there's no need to worry about fraying edges. Here it's used to make an appliance cover with a simple design.

1 ▶ Measure the dimensions of the kitchen appliance to be covered and cut rectangles of thick felt for front and back, plus top and side panels.

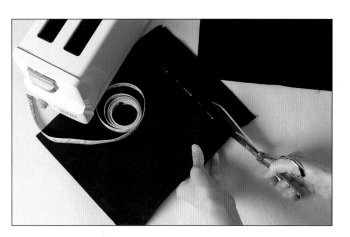

2 ◀ Trace the bird pattern on page 156 and cut out the sections of the tracing. Use these as templates to cut pieces in felt. Arrange the felt pieces on the base felt and pin them in place.

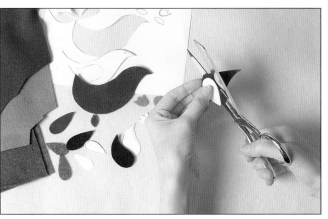

3 ◀ Secure each piece of the motif with overcasting stitches using two strands of embroidery thread. Sew the stems of the flowers in stem stitch (see page 123).

4 ▶ Assemble the panels of the cover and sew them together with well-spaced buttonhole stitches, using three strands of stranded cotton.

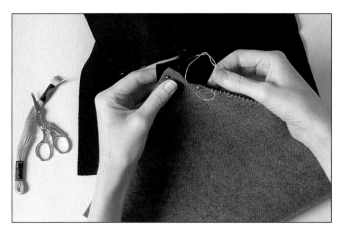

PROJECT 17

Apron

These cheeky cats will keep a child great company as he or she helps out in the kitchen. Size the apron to fit the intended recipient.

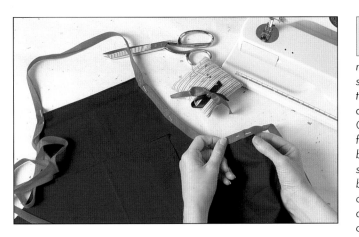

1 ◄ *Enlarge the apron pattern on page 157 to a suitable size (see page 12 for more on this). Fold a piece of strong fabric in half and lay the paper template so that the dashed line is along the fold. Cut the apron and a rectangle for a pocket. Hem along the base and the straight top and side sections. Pin a length of bias binding along the arm curves to form a neck loop and ties. Sew the bias binding onto the apron.*

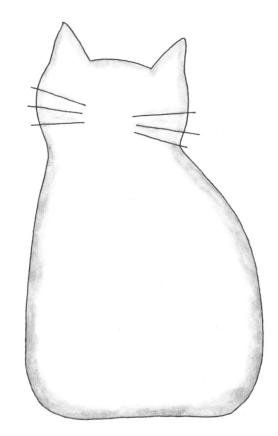

2 ▲ *Trace the cat pattern onto the backing paper on fusible webbing. Lay the webbing, glue side down, onto the wrong side of fabric scraps. Iron to fix, following the manufacturer's instructions. Cut the cat shapes from the fabric scraps.*

3 ► *Peel off the backing paper and arrange the cats on the apron. Fix them in position with an iron. Using two strands of stranded cotton, sew large buttonhole stitches around each cat. Stitch the whiskers in straight stitches using four strands. Sew the pocket in place.*

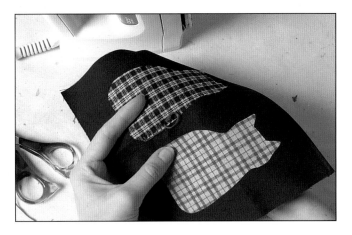

PROJECT 18

Pin Keepsake

Dyed and appliquéd, inexpensive lace can be made very special. Here it adorns an heirloom cushion decorated with pins, traditionally given to welcome a baby.

YOU WILL NEED
lace
satin fabric
sheer top fabric
rust-proof pins
anti-fraying liquid
sawdust or bran
sewing equipment

1 ▶ For an old-fashioned look, dye white lace by dipping it in coffee or tea, rinsing it in cold water and leaving it to dry. Apply anti-fray liquid to the edge of motifs and then carefully cut them out.

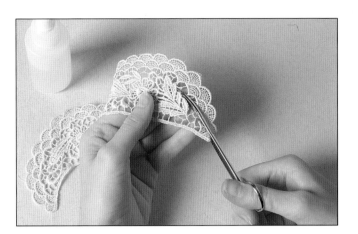

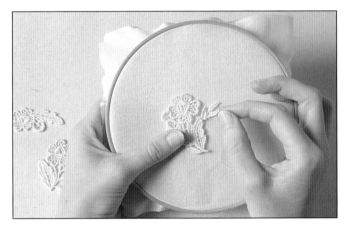

2 ◀ Cut a square of satin base fabric and a matching piece of sheer top fabric. Position the lace motifs on the layered fabrics and stitch them in place with a matching thread and tiny stitches.

3 ▶ Mark and baste a circle around the appliqué, then lay it face down on backing fabric. Sew around the basting, stitching all the layers together, but leave a gap for turning. Trim the edges and turn the cushion right side out. Sew a trim of lace around the edge.

4 ◀ Fill the cushion with sawdust or bran, which will hold pins firmly in place, and handsew the opening closed. Push rust-proof pins into the cushion, highlighting the design of the lace. Note: the cushion is an heirloom, not a baby's toy!

Quilting

The technique of quilting, joining layers of fabric together with stitching, often goes hand in hand with the craft of quilt-making and the two terms are often used interchangeably. Certainly, the former is a necessary part of the latter, but not necessarily the other way round.

There are three parts to a quilted work: the decorative top layer which might include patchwork or appliqué, the middle part which is the wadding, and the third part – the backing. These three sections are held together by quilting stitches, which can be an important decorative feature in their own right.

Before printed fabrics became available in the eighteenth century, plain fabrics were quilted with elaborate designs to create soft furnishings and clothes such as hats and waistcoats. Hand quilting continued to flourish in isolated areas, where particular designs and motifs became a local tradition.

The most commonly used stitch in quilting is the running stitch, with its characteristic broken line. For a more pronounced line, back stitch can be used, or other linear stitches such as the chain stitch. If you are stitching a design, however, the stitches should not be allowed to dominate. Try to work stitches of an even length.

Choose a smooth, natural-fiber fabric for the top layer, such as cotton, silk, or a cotton and wool blend. A quilting design will be less visible on patterned fabrics and will show up best on pale colors. Wadding or batting is available in cotton, wool, synthetics, or a blend of these, and in different thicknesses. For the backing, use a soft cotton or sheeting. The thread should be strong; specially made quilting threads are available, although in a limited color range.

A hoop is useful for holding the layers taut while you work. A quilter's pencil marks a fine line and should be kept sharp. Short needles known as betweens are most suitable.

Quilting can be as simple a matter as these long basting stitches, used to hold the wadding in place in a mat. Wadding or batting provides insulation, so it is useful for any project designed to give warmth or protection.

Simple repeat patterns can be used on plain fabrics or in conjunction with patchwork and appliqué techniques.

Quilting can be worked quickly with the aid of a sewing machine, especially if the quilting lines are straight. Use masking tape to help create regular parallel lines.

In trapunto and Italian cording techniques, extra body is added to sections of the work. If the top fabric is sheer, the color of the padding can become part of the design.

PROJECT 19

Pot Holder

YOU WILL NEED
cotton fabrics
backing fabric
wadding
strong thread
tracing paper
a marker
masking tape
binding
sewing equipment

*This small project is ideal for those new to quilting.
It can be worked quickly with scrap fabric and creates
a useful and attractive item for the kitchen.*

1 Trace the pattern and then carefully cut out one 'petal' from the tracing. Transfer the pattern onto a square of cotton fabric, by repeatedly rotating the tracing and drawing along the edge of the hole.

2 Cut the fabric into a square of the desired size. Cut matching pieces of wadding and another piece of cotton and stack them with the design on top. Pin the layers. Knot a length of strong cotton thread at one end and sew a series of small running stitches along the design lines, working outwards wherever possible.

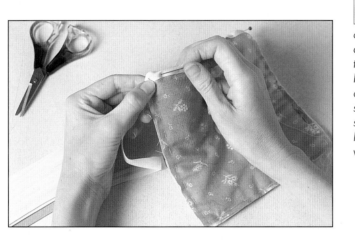

3 Cut a backing section from strong fabric and lay the quilted square on top. Baste along the edges, securing all the layers. Fold and pin a length of binding tape or ribbon around the edge, allowing extra at one corner to form a hanging loop. Stitch along the binding, securing all layers neatly.

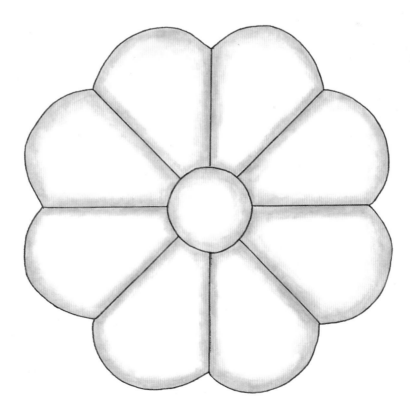

PROJECT 20

Quilted Bib

This stunning bib would make a lovely baby's gift for use on very special occasions. For safety, make sure the beads are securely attached.

YOU WILL NEED
cotton fabric
backing fabric
thin wadding
perlé thread
paper & a marker
masking tape
beads
ribbon
an embroidery hoop
sewing equipment

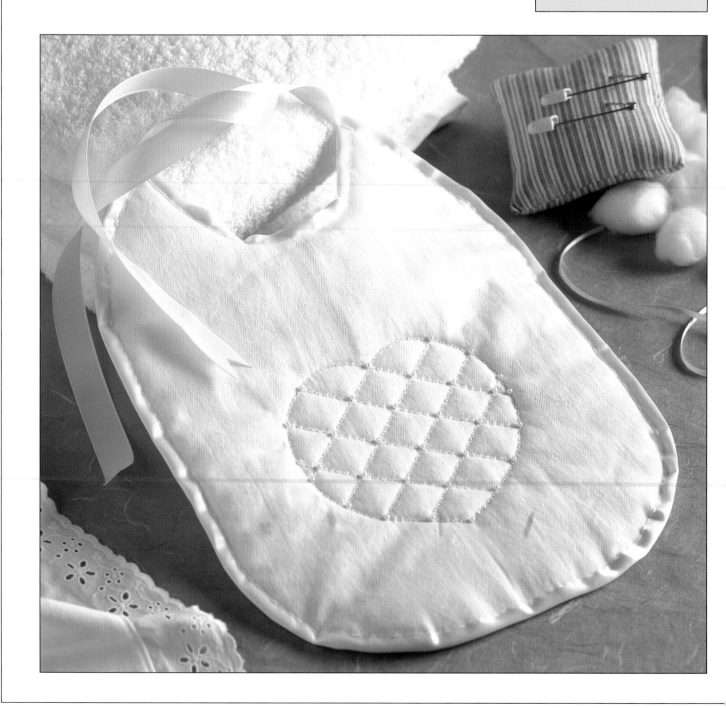

1 ▶ Fold a sheet of paper in half and trace the pattern on page 157 so that the dotted line is along the fold. Cut the folded paper to create a bib template. Mark the outline on cotton fabric and then mark the heart shape. Cut around the bib outline, then cut wadding and backing fabric the same size and pin the layers together.

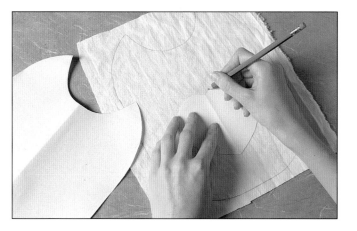

2 ▶ Place in an embroidery hoop. Lay parallel strips of masking tape diagonally across the heart. Knot a length of perlé thread at one end and stitch a series of running stitches along the edges of the tape. Turn the tape strips to create a diamond pattern and stitch the remaining quilting lines.

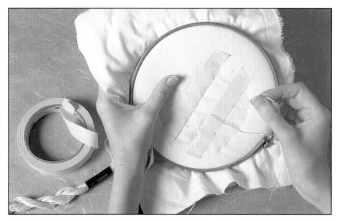

3 ▶ Remove the tape and quilt the heart outline. Stitch a small bead securely at the intersection of each diamond, running the thread through the wadding between diamonds, so it does not show at the back.

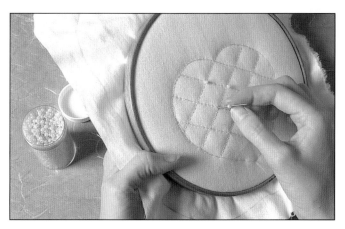

4 ▶ Remove the work from the hoop and press gently around the beaded design. Baste around the bib outline and trim the work neatly. Pin a length of ribbon around the bib, allowing for ties, and handsew the folded ribbon so that it binds the edges of the bib.

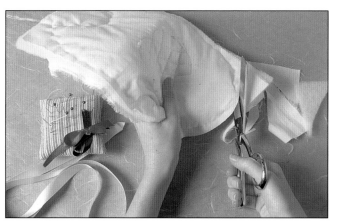

PROJECT 21

Cosmetic Bag

This project draws on Italian quilting, where yarn is threaded through quilted channels. A sheer top fabric adds subtle color to the dimensional effect.

1 Cut two pieces of sheer cotton fabric and a piece of thin wadding, each 9 x 5½ ". Transfer the pattern below onto one piece of fabric.

2 Lay the wadding between the pieces of fabric and baste the layers together around the edges. Choose a suitable color of stranded cotton. Knot a single strand at one end and sew a series of small running stitches along the lines of the pattern.

3 When quilting is complete, thread a blunt needle with tapestry wool. Working from the back, insert the needle through the base fabric and the wadding but do not pierce the top fabric. Run the needle along a quilted channel, bring it out again at the back, and trim both ends close to the fabric. Repeat this, running parallel stitches of wool to fill (but not overfill) the quilted channels. Once complete, use the needle to hook the ends inside the work.

4 Lay a 7 " zip along the top edge of the stitched section, right sides facing, and sew. Cut a matching piece of fabric and sew the other side of the zip in place. Open the zip and sew the sides of the bag, right sides facing. Turn the bag right side out. Make a lining bag, insert it, and handsew the lining to the bag.

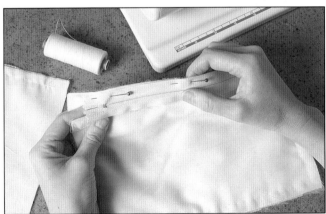

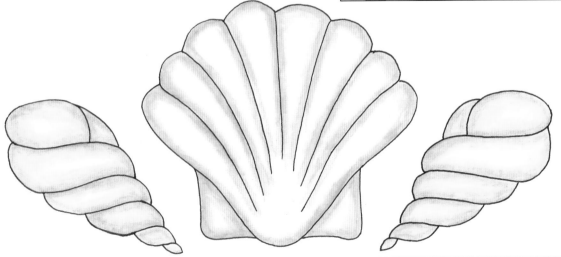

Cut & Drawn

Just as silence can play an important part in music, openwork – where areas of the fabric are missing – can be an important element in embroidery. There are several types of openwork. The threads of a fabric can be pulled and distorted with certain stitches, or they can be selectively removed and the remaining ones rearranged. These two techniques are suitable for decorating loose, evenly woven fabrics, where the distortion makes a greater impact. Cutwork, where sections of the fabric are cut away in a design, can be worked on various fabrics, although they should have a close weave to reduce fraying.

Cutwork was especially popular in Italy and Scandinavia in the seventeenth and eighteenth centuries when intricate examples resembled needlemade lace. It is worked by outlining a simple motif with running stitch and then with buttonhole stitch before cutting away the fabric inside the motif. In more complex forms of cutwork, the cut-away areas are decorated with a tracery of bars or ornamental loops known as 'picots'.

Working cutwork by hand can be a time-consuming task and many people will prefer to use a sewing machine. You may need to back your work with a commercial fabric stabilizer, especially when machining light-weight fabrics.

Drawn threadwork is one of the most delicate embroidery styles. Threads are pulled out in bands from the fabric and stitches are worked to pull some of the remaining warp or weft threads together in clusters. The result is a formal but delicate effect. This type of embroidery originated in Europe during the sixteenth century and was mainly worked by peasants who used it to decorate costumes. Today it is more common on table linen, napkins, guest towels and handkerchiefs as it does not fare well when washed regularly in a machine. Threads of the same color as the fabric should be used for hemming the edges and adding decoration to drawn work, as a contrasting color can distract from the general effect.

Two examples of intricate cutwork: broderie anglaise and a collar with delicate lattice work.

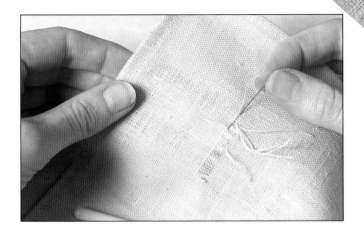

For drawn thread
▲ projects, remove a
number of parallel
threads from the ground
fabric. Do this with an
unpicker, starting in the
middle and working out-
wards. Secure the ends of the
drawn area either by weaving
each loose thread back into
the fabric, as shown here, or
by working close buttonhole
stitches along the edge.

This napkin includes both
drawn threadwork – the
hemstitched borders –
and some pulled work –
the large eye stitch below
the cross-stitching.

Traditionally, cutwork is
formed with the same color
thread as the fabric, but a
careful design can employ
strong colors to good effect.

PROJECT 22

Scallop Edging

This old-fashioned edging requires a little patience, but will add an elegant touch to a special nightdress, bed linen or a tablecloth.

1 ▶ Fold paper, concertina fashion, to the desired width of the scallop. Draw a curve evenly across the front section, using a compass if necessary. Cut along the curve and unfold the paper strip. Lay this along the edge of the fabric and mark the border. Raise the strip slightly and mark the second series of curves.

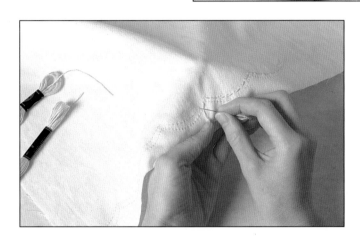

2 ▶ Using the full six strands of thread, stitch along both outlines with a series of small running stitches. Between the outlines, baste two rows of long stitches, which will give the edging extra body.

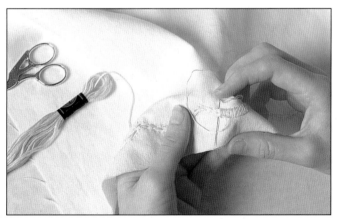

3 ◀ Cut a long piece of variegated stranded cotton and separate it into sets of two strands. Thread a sharp needle with two strands and secure it between the outlines. Work a series of very close button-hole stitches (see page 123) with the loops at the edge that will be cut away.

4 ◀ Once the stitching is complete, carefully cut away the outer fabric close to the stitching, preferably with a small pair of curved scissors.

PROJECT 23

Drawn Cloth

YOU WILL NEED
evenweave fabric
stranded cotton
an unpicker
a blunt needle
sewing equipment

In this drawn thread project, clusters of cross-threads are twisted at intervals to produce a delicate effect which is ideal for table linen.

1 Cut and hem evenweave fabric to the desired size. Plan where you want the decoration. Remove a band of parallel threads with an unpicker. Secure the ends of the drawn area either by weaving each loose thread back into the fabric or by working close buttonhole stitches along the edge.

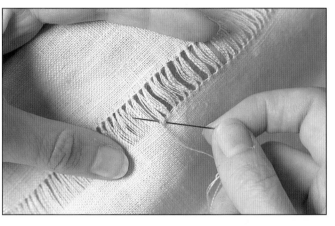

2 Hem one side of the drawn area as follows. Secure the sewing thread, pick up four fabric threads on the needle, pull through and then encircle those four threads. Stitch two threads deep into the hem and bring the needle out after the encircled cluster. Hem the other side so that the clusters match.

3 Cut a length of stranded cotton slightly longer than the drawn area. Secure the stranded cotton at one end of the drawn area. Pass over two clusters and pick up the second cluster with the needle coming back towards you.

4 Twist the needle and insert it behind the first cluster, working away from you once more. Bring the needle through to the front, pull the thread taut and work the next two clusters as before. At the end of the drawn area, secure the central thread neatly.

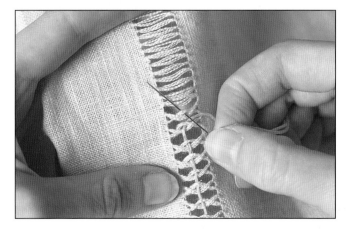

PROJECT 24

Potpourri Sachet

In this project, only one layer of fabric is cut. The cutwork adds a pretty touch and the scent of potpourri can escape through the sheer lining.

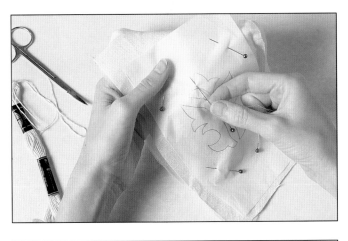

1 Trace the design onto a piece of tissue paper. Cut two 9½ x 5 " pieces of cotton and two matching pieces of sheer lining. Pin the tracing on a cotton piece with lining behind it and sew along the lines of the design with small running stitches in a single strand of thread.

2 Gently tear away the tissue paper, leaving the running stitches in place. Using two strands of thread, stitch around the design with close buttonhole stitches so that the loops of the stitches lie along the edge to be cut.

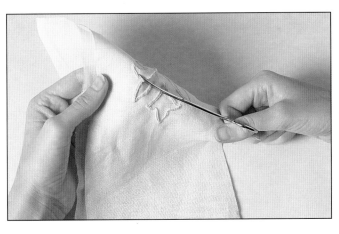

3 With a pair of small scissors (preferably curved ones), cut away the top fabric in the stitched areas. Take great care not to pierce the lining fabric. Baste the remaining fabric pieces together for the back of the sachet.

4 Lay the front and back sections together, right sides facing. Seam around the sides and base, leaving 1½ " unsewn at the top on either side. Turn right side out. Turn the opening of the top fabric and lining in and sew them together 1 " down from the opening. Make a cord from stranded cotton (see page 15). Fill the sachet with potpourri and tie the cord loosely around the neck.

Basic Knitting

Knitting is an age-old method of making fabric by creating interlocking loops of yarn using a pair of needles. It is very easy to learn as there are only two basic stitches: knit and purl. To begin, a row of stitches is cast onto one needle and the stitches are then transferred one at a time to the other needle. The methods of transferring each stitch and winding the yarn around the needles creates the textural pattern.

Sheep's wool is the traditional knitting yarn, but other natural fibers such as cottons and special wools (mohair, for example) are available, as are synthetics with various textures. Knitting yarns are usually classified by the number of plys twisted together to make a strand. Always try to obtain the yarn recommended when knitting from a pattern and always buy enough yarn to complete your project as dye lots can vary.

Needles come in a variety of sizes but, until you're experienced, work with the size called for in the pattern.

Once you have the right wool and needles you can start knitting. You will need to watch the gauge or tightness of your work, to make sure that it is even. When knitting a garment, it is important to match the gauge recommended by the pattern; if you are knitting too tightly, your garment will be too small. Change to larger needles and test again until you get it right. If your knitting is too loose, switch to needles a size smaller. Basic knitting stitches are outlined on pages 80-1.

Some work, especially stockinette stitch, may need to be blocked and pressed before sections can be sewn together; see page 13 for more detail. Pressing rib or garter stitch knits, however, will spoil their elasticity. Sew seams together with back stitch using a blunt needle and matching wool.

Gauge is measured by counting the number of stitches and rows you knit to a given measurement.

Most projects are worked with a pair of single-pointed needles. They range in size from 0 to 15.

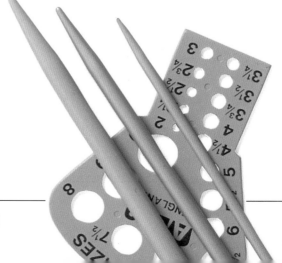

ABBREVIATIONS

There are many abbreviations used for knitting terms. Here are the ones used for projects in this book.

dec	decrease
inc	increase
K	knit
K2 tog	knit 2 stitches together
rep	repeat
P	purl
P2 tog	purl 2 stitches together
psso	pass the slipped stitch over the last stitch worked and off the needle
yo	bring yarn forward and over
sl	slip the next stitch across to the right needle without working it
st(s)	stitch(es)

Stockinette stitch is formed by knitting one row and purling the next. It stretches horizontally.

Garter stitch is formed when every row is knitted; the resulting work is very elastic.

Many wonderful patterns can be knitted by combining stitches. However, even the two basic patterns mentioned above can be shaped into intriguing figures.

Stitch markers and a row counter (which fits onto a knitting needle) can be great aids, especially when working complex patterns.

Knitting Instructions

To the uninitiated, a knitting pattern can look like an early form of computer programming. However, once you have learned the common abbreviations (see the previous page), you'll find that patterns are generally quite simple to follow.

Instructions often include parentheses and asterisks, indicating sections that need to be repeated. Parentheses will be followed by a number indicating how many times to repeat a sequence.

The instructions below are devised for right-handed people. Left-handed knitters should reverse the pictures in a mirror.

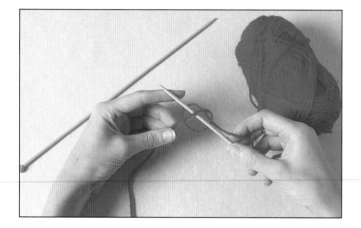

Slip Knot

◀ *A slip knot is the starting point for knitting and counts as the first stitch when casting on. Wrap the long end of the yarn around the short end and lift the main strand through the loop with your needle. Pull on the main end to tighten the knot.*

Casting On (1 needle)

▶ *Make a slip knot some distance from the end of the yarn (leaving enough to work the first row). Hold the needle in your right hand with the main yarn wound around those fingers. Hold the short end with your left hand as shown. Insert the needle through the loop around your thumb. Wrap the main yarn under and over the needle point and draw the yarn through onto the needle to form a stitch. Tighten the yarn and wind it around your thumb again, ready for the next stitch.*

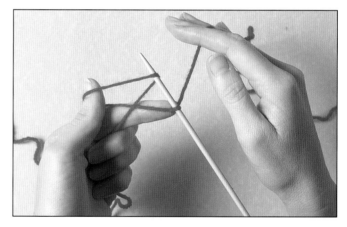

Casting On (2 needles)

▶ *Make a slip knot a short distance from the end of the yarn. Hold the needle with the slip knot in your left hand and the empty needle in your right hand, with the main yarn wound around those fingers. Insert the right needle into the slip knot from the front to the back and take the yarn under and around the needle point. Draw the yarn through the slip knot to form a new stitch and put this onto the left-hand needle. For further stitches, insert the right-hand needle into the new stitch each time.*

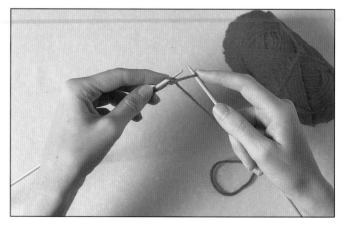

Knit

▶ Hold the needle with the existing stitches in your left hand and the working needle and yarn in your right. Insert the working needle through the first stitch on the left needle, from front to back. Bring the yarn forward, under and over the right needle. Draw the yarn through onto the right needle, allowing the old stitch to slip off the left needle. One stitch has been knitted (K1).

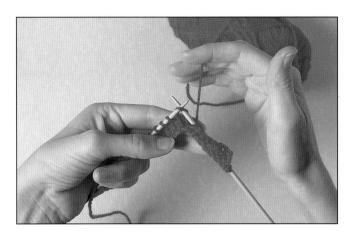

Purl

▶ Hold the needles and yarn as for knitting, but with the yarn at the front of your work. Insert the working needle from right to left through the front of the first stitch on the left needle. Wrap the yarn counter-clockwise around the right needle and then between the needles. Draw the yarn through onto the right needle, allowing the old stitch to slip off the left needle. One stitch has been purled (P1).

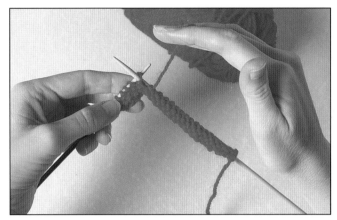

Increasing

Increasing and decreasing can be used to shape work and also to create certain patterns. There are several methods of increasing. A stitch can be knitted twice, a technique often used at the edges of the work. Bringing the yarn forward in the middle of a row is used when working lacy patterns. Knitting between the stitches, by picking up a loop and knitting it as if it were a stitch, is the most invisible method of increasing.

Decreasing

There are two basic methods for decreasing. You can insert the right needle into two stitches at the same time and knit (or purl) them together. Alternatively, you can pass a slip stitch over, by slipping a stitch onto the right needle without working it, knitting the next stitch and then passing the slipped stitch over the last one worked and off the needle.

Binding Off

▶ Always bind off in the pattern you are working. If it should be a knitting row, knit the first two stitches then * use the left needle to lift the first stitch over the second and off the needle. Knit the next stitch and repeat from * until only one stitch remains. Cut the yarn, leaving a short tail, and draw this through the last stitch on the needle. If it should be a purl row, follow the earlier instructions, but replace knit with purl.

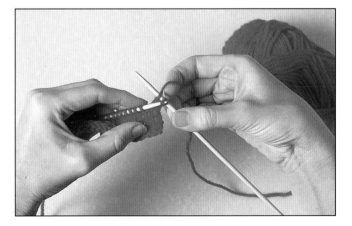

PROJECT 25

Lacy Scarf

YOU WILL NEED
soft wool
size 10 needles
a row counter
scissors
a blunt needle

The mesh lace scarf pictured is knitted with angora, which is beautifully soft against the skin. However, a less fluffy yarn would show off the pattern to better effect.

1 Cast on 31 stitches, using either method. Knit the basic pattern as follows:
Row 1: K1, * yo, sl 1, K1, psso, K1, K2 tog, yo, K1, rep from * to end.
Row 2: Purl.
Row 3: K1, * yo, K1, sl 1, K2 tog, psso, K1, yo, K1, rep from * to end.
Row 4: Purl.

2 Row 5: K1, * K2 tog, yo, K1, yo, sl 1, K1, psso, K1, rep from * to end.
Row 6: Purl.
Row 7: K2 tog, * (K1, yo) twice, K1, sl 1, K2 tog, psso, rep from * until last 5 sts, then (K1, yo) twice, K1, sl 1, K1, psso.
Row 8: Purl.
Repeat these 8 rows until the scarf is the desired length.

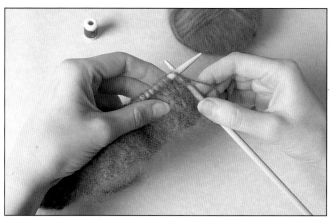

3 Bind off on a purl row. Cut the yarn twice the desired fringe length. Insert a crochet hook or latchhook though the scarf's edge and catch two lengths of yarn in the middle. Pull them halfway through, then catch the loose ends and pull them through the loop. Repeat this along the edge and then trim the fringe neatly.

PROJECT 26

Baby Boots

A pair of booties is an essential element in any baby's wardrobe. These would make a delightful gift on the baby's arrival or to mark a christening.

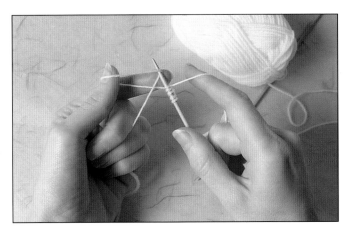

1 ◄ Cast on 20 stitches. Work 8 rows of garter stitch, increasing 1 st at the beginning of each row. Work 8 more rows, decreasing 1 st at the beginning of every row. This will be the boot sole.

2 ◄ Row 17: cast on an extra 5 sts for the heel and then K the row, changing to stockinette stitch from here.
Row 18: Inc 1, purl to end. Work next 6 rows, increasing 1 st at the beginning of every purl row, to give 29 sts.
Row 25: Bind off 10 sts, K19.
Row 26: P17, P2 tog.
Row 27: K2 tog, K16.
Row 28: P15, P2 tog.
Work 6 rows without shaping.
Row 35: Inc 1, K16.

Row 36: P17, inc 1.
Row 37: Inc 1, K18.
Row 38: P19.
Row 39: Cast on 10 sts, K19.
Row 40: Dec 1, P to end. Knit the next row and continue, decreasing 1 at the beginning of every purl row until 25 sts remain. Bind off.

3 ► Press the work lightly. With the right side of the work facing, pick up 30 sts from around the ankle edge and work the frill:
Row 1: K1, * yo, K1, rep from * to end, giving 59 sts.
Row 2: Knit.
Row 3: K1, * yo, K2 tog, rep from * to end.
Bind off. Work another boot, reversing the shaping.

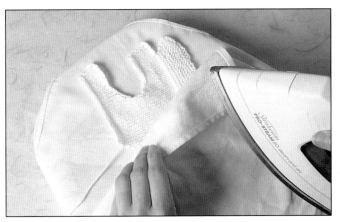

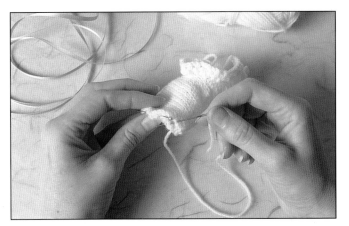

4 ◄ Sew the sole and heel seams with a flat seam. Thread a narrow ribbon through the holes in the base of the frill and tie it in a bow once the boot is on the baby's foot.

PROJECT 27

Aran Throw

YOU WILL NEED
size 7 needles
8 ply cream wool
scissors
a blunt needle

Textural patterns knitted in thick creamy wool are traditional on the Aran Isles off Ireland. These two designs say much of island life, where religion and the sea's harvest are all important.

1 ▶ To make a trinity square: Cast on 34 sts by the one-needle method. Knit 6 rows and then:
Row 1: K3, P to last 3 sts, K3.
Row 2: K3, * (K1, P1, K1) into next st, P3 tog. Rep from * to last 3 sts, K3.
Row 3: as 1st row.
Row 4: K3, * P3 tog (K1, P1, K1) all into next st. Rep from * to last 3 sts, K3.
Rep these 4 rows 8 times more, K7 rows, then bind off.

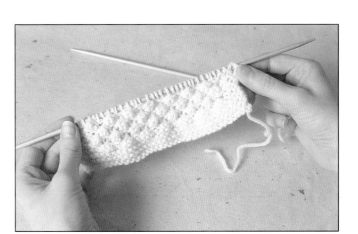

2 ◀ To make a fisherman's net square: Cast on 34 sts by the one needle method and K6 rows, inc 1 st in center of the last row, then:
Row 1: K7, then (P1, K7) 3 times, P1, K3.
Row 2: K3, P1, K1, (P5, K1, P1, K1) 3 times, P3, K3.
Row 3: K5, (P1, K3) to last 6 sts, P1, K5.
Row 4: K3, P3, (K1, P1, K1, P5) 3 times, K1, P1, K3.
Row 5: K3, then (P1, K7) 3 times, P1, K7.
Row 6: as Row 4.
Row 7: as Row 3.
Row 8: As Row 2.
Rep these 8 rows 3 more times, then the first 5 rows again. K6 rows, dec 1 st in center of 1st row. Bind off.

3 ▶ Knit as many squares as you require, working the different patterns in even numbers. Lay the squares out in an alternating pattern, with the garter stitch rows aligned. Using a flat seam, join a series of squares into a strip. Then sew the strips together.

4 ◀ If the stitched squares are distorted, block the throw by pinning down the work squarely with rust-proof pins, laying a damp cloth on top and pressing it lightly with a warm iron.

Color Knits

While there are many beautiful textural patterns to knit in a single color, you will soon want to introduce other colors into your work. There are several ways in which this can be achieved.

Stripes are one of the easiest methods, as you simply join a new yarn at the start of a row, weaving the loose ends into the work later. When two colors are used in the same row, as in Fair Isle patterns, you may need to carry the wool across the back. These loose yarns can be snagged and create uneven tension, so they need to be woven into the back of the work every few stitches. This is done as you knit, by twisting the two yarns regularly.

Jacquard patterns involve more than two colors in a row, requiring at least two yarns to be woven in at the back.

When knitting a design which includes small isolated patches of color, you may find it helpful to use bobbins to hold small amounts of yarn. This reduces the likelihood of tangling. The yarn not in use is not carried across the back, but you must twist the yarns each time a new block of color is reached. This step, called intarsia, prevents holes from forming where the blocks of color meet.

Complex multicolored designs can be worked from a chart, much as you would work cross-stitch or needlepoint, with each square of the chart corresponding to a stitch in the knitting. If a pattern is printed in black and white, symbols will often be used to represent different colors. If you are designing your own patterns or motifs, keep in mind that a stitch in a stockinette stitch work is not quite square and this will add some distortion. For example, a square motif will become a slightly squat rectangle.

Another approach to adding color is to add stitches to a completed knit, similar to embroidery. Swiss darning (or duplicate stitch) is one method, explored in Project 28. Other stitches can be used to add a pattern rather than a motif.

Multicolored yarns can be used to add color quickly and easily. This knitting is worked in stripes, including some knitted with flexible viscose ribbon.

Once a garment or item has been knitted, extra stitching can be added using a needle. This is especially simple with items worked in stockinette stitch. For applied decoration like this and Swiss darning, use the same weight of wool as that used to originally knit the item.

Fair Isle patterns developed on the Shetland Island of that name, but they probably originated in Spain and were brought to the island by ship-wrecked sailors. Traditionally, Fair Isle garments were knitted in the round, as this scarf has been worked.

The tea cosy in Project 30 is worked by weaving yarns at the back, but could have been made by the intarsia method.

PROJECT 28

Swiss Darning

YOU WILL NEED
a knitted garment
colored wool
a blunt needle
scissors

Swiss darning is a wonderful way to brighten up a plain stockinette stitch garment with scraps of wool. This little floral motif takes only a minute or two to stitch.

1 ▶ Select a stockinette stitch knitted garment. Those shown are loosely knit; the motif will be smaller on a tighter knit. Thread a blunt needle with wool the same thickness as the garment. With right side facing, bring the needle out at the base of the first stitch. Insert the needle behind the two threads of the stitch above.

2 ▶ Draw the needle through, leaving a tail at the back. Insert the needle into the base of the stitch again to complete a stitch. Repeat this with adjoining stitches in the same row, then move to the next row and work in the opposite direction.

3 ▶ When all stitches in one color are completed, secure the yarn at the back. Thread the needle with the next color and work stitches as shown in the chart.

4 ▶ On the inside of the garment, secure the loose ends of wool behind the stitches and trim neatly. Work as many motifs as you like, either randomly or in a counted arrangement.

PROJECT 29

Scented Pillows

YOU WILL NEED
8 ply wool
size 5 needles
scissors
a blunt needle
spiced potpourri
fiber filler
ribbon

This snowflake is a traditional design in Scandinavian knitting. When worked in bright Christmas colors, it makes a charming scented decoration.

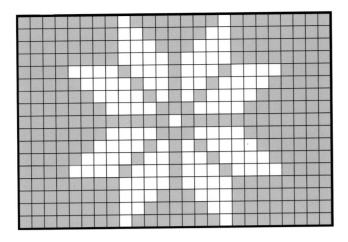

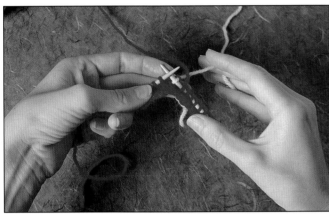

1 Cast on 25 stitches in red yarn, using the two-needle method. Working in stockinette stitch, knit four rows. In the 5th row, K8 red, then join in white yarn for one stitch. K7 red, weaving the white yarn across the back, then K1 white, K8 red. This is the first row of the chart.

2 Continue knitting in stockinette stitch, changing colors according to the chart. Weave the yarn not in use across the back, catching it up every second or third stitch. After the last row of the pattern, cut the white yarn and continue in red, working 4 rows and then binding off. Knit a matching back section.

3 Press each side lightly and lay them together, right sides facing. Seam along three edges and turn the pillow right side out. Place a spoonful of potpourri scented with cloves and cinnamon into a wad of fiber filler. Insert the filler in the knitted pillow. Fix a loop of ribbon at one corner and stitch the opening closed.

PROJECT 30

Teapot Cozy

YOU WILL NEED
8 ply wool
size 7 needles
scissors
a blunt needle

This checkered cozy will add a nostalgic touch to your table, as well as a hint of color. The pattern is designed to fit a small teapot.

1 ▶ Cast on 42 stitches in color A, using the one-needle method.
Rows 1 and 2: K in color A
Row 3: P1A, * K5B, P2A, rep from * to last 6 sts, K5B, P1A
As you work, weave the yarn not in use across at the back.

2 ◀ Row 4: Purl, picking up the same colors for each stitch as used in the previous row.
Rows 5 - 8: rep 3rd and 4th rows twice.
Row 9: rep 3rd row, using only color A.
Row 10: Knit in A.

3 ▶ Repeat Rows 1 to 10 three times. From this point, only use color A.
Next row: K2, * yo, K2 tog, K1, K2 tog, rep from * to end of row, giving 34 sts.
Knit 6 rows and then bind off. Work a second matching section. Press lightly with a damp cloth and a warm iron.

4 ▶ Sew up the sides with a flat seam, leaving gaps for the teapot's spout and handle. Cut a 2 yard length of of yarn A and another of B. Fold each in half and loop them, then make a twisted cord (see page 17). Thread this through the holes in the top of the cozy and trim it to a suitable length.

Crochet

Apart from its origins, there is very little mystery to the craft of crochet: all you need is a hook and some yarn. Indeed, the word *crochet* is French for 'hook'.

Crochet is thought to have originated among nomadic tribes of Africa and Asia. It has been worked in the Middle East for many centuries. In Europe, it developed as a means of emulating fine lace produced in the Middle Ages and in the sixteenth century it was used to create trimmings for church cloths and vestments. By the nineteenth century, it had become a more popular craft and was often known as 'shepherd's knitting'. The income derived from crochet work helped many Irish families survive the great famine of the 1840s, and many beautiful designs were created during this period.

Crochet hooks are available in a wide range of sizes. The smaller ones tend to be made of steel, the larger ones of wood or plastic. Traditionally, hooks were turned from bone. The hook size and the weight of the yarn selected for a project are related and together they determine the result. Fine cotton thread, purpose made, can be crocheted into delicate lacy edgings, doilies, jug covers, and so on. Wool, worked with a medium-sized hook, can be crocheted into clothing or afghan bedspreads. The largest hooks can be used in conjunction with rope or cotton rags to make rugs. Even raffia and string can be crocheted.

Only a handful of stitches need to be learned before you can work from crochet patterns. Instructions for these can be found on pages 98–99.

Most crochet has gaps between stitches, but continuous single crochet has a solid appearance.

Crochet cottons are available in a range of lovely pastel colors which suit delicate projects.

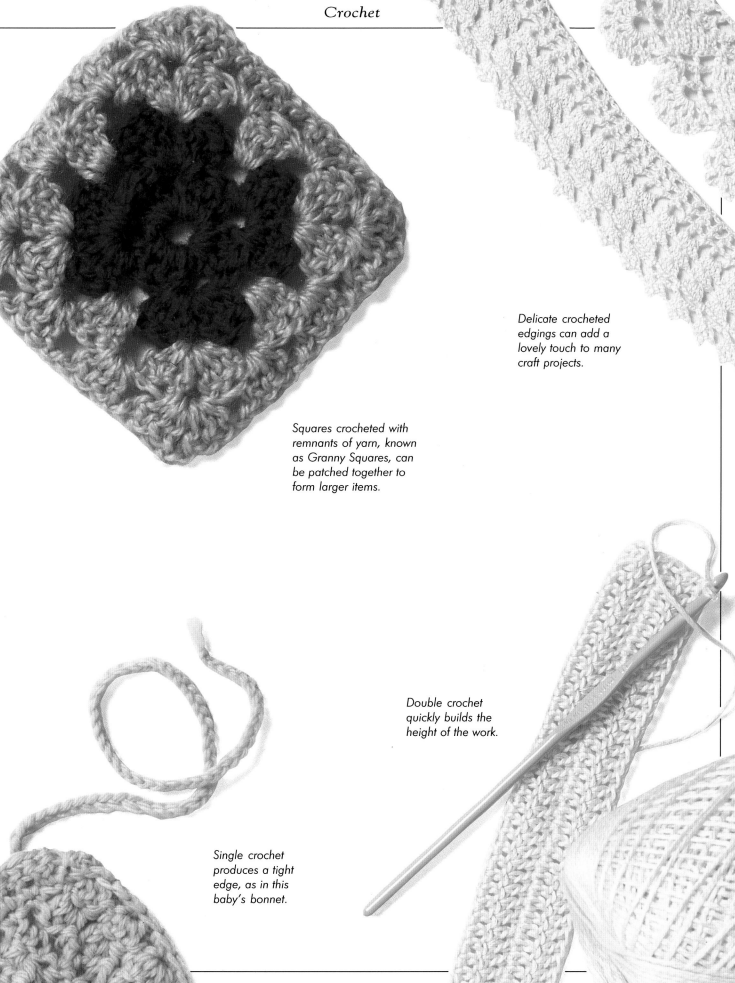

Delicate crocheted edgings can add a lovely touch to many craft projects.

Squares crocheted with remnants of yarn, known as Granny Squares, can be patched together to form larger items.

Double crochet quickly builds the height of the work.

Single crochet produces a tight edge, as in this baby's bonnet.

Crochet Instructions

Crochet stitches are formed simply by pulling a loop of yarn through another. The five basic stitches shown below can be combined to create various patterns. Singles, doubles and trebles all add height in varying degrees, while slip stitch moves along the row horizontally. Parentheses and asterisks are used in patterns to indicate sequences which should be repeated.

Left-handed people may find it helpful to reverse the pictures in a mirror.

Start your crochet work with a slip knot (see page 80) looped onto the crochet hook.

Chain (ch)

 This is the basis for all crochet work. Once a slip knot is made, wrap the yarn over the hook (yo). Draw the yarn through the loop on the hook to make a new loop. Repeat this until the chain is the desired length.

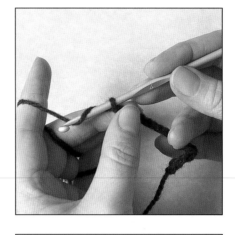

Turning chain (tch)

At the start of each row, one or more chain stitches are required to establish the height of the new row. These turning chains form the first stitch of each row.

Single (sc)

 1 Insert the hook under the top loop of the next stitch.

 2 Wrap the yarn over the hook (yo) and draw it through the work only. Yo and draw it through both loops on the hook.

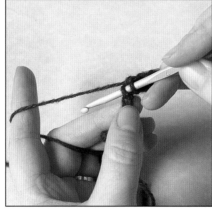

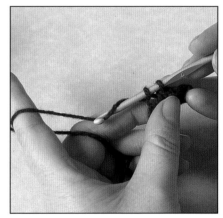

Double (dc)

 1 Wrap the yarn over the hook (yo). Insert the hook under the top loop of the next stitch and draw the yarn through the work only.

 2 Yo and then draw it through the next two loops on the hook. Yo and draw it through the remaining two loops on the hook.

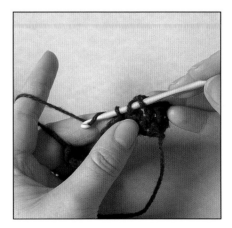

Treble (tr)

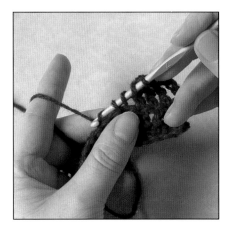

1 ▶ Wrap yarn over hook (yo) twice. Insert the hook under the top loop of the next stitch, yo and draw the yarn through the work only.

2 ▶ Yo and then draw it through the next two loops on the hook.

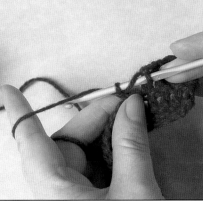

3 ▶ Yo and draw it through the next two loops on the hook.

4 ▶ Yo and draw it through the last two loops on the hook.

Slip (sl)

▶ Insert the hook under the top loop of the next stitch. Wrap the yarn over the hook and draw the yarn through both the work and the loop on the hook in one movement.

Fastening off

▶ Prevent the work from unraveling by fastening it off securely. After the last stitch, make one more chain and pull it into a large loop. Cut the yarn and continue to pull the loose end right through the chain. Sew all loose ends into the work with a large blunt needle.

PROJECT 31

Ring Pillow

Add extra romance to the wedding day with a lacy pillow for the rings. For everyday uses, crochet edgings are also pretty on handkerchiefs and washers.

YOU WILL NEED

size 8 crochet hook
fine crochet cotton
a blunt needle
sheer fabric
polyester filler
narrow ribbon
sewing equipment

1 Cut two squares of sheer fabric and lay them right sides together. Seam around the edges, leaving a gap at one side for turning. Turn the pillow right side out and fill it with polyester filler. Handsew the opening closed. Measure the perimeter of the pillow.

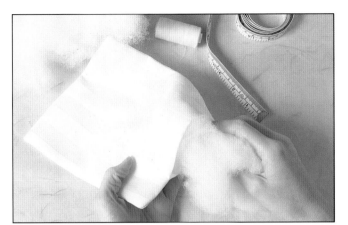

2 Crochet chain in multiples of four, plus one, to the measurement of the pillow's perimeter.
First row: 1 tch, 1 row sc.
Second row: 4 tch, 3 ch, 1 tr into fourth sc, * 3 ch, 1 tr, repeat from * to end of row.

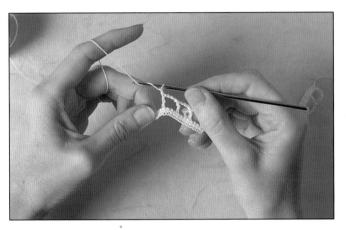

3 Third row: 1 tch, * skip 1 ch, 4 dc into next ch, skip 1 ch, 1 sl into tr, repeat from * to end of row.
Fasten off and sew in loose threads. Press gently.

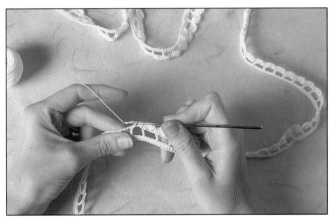

4 Pin the edging around the pillow and handsew it in position with small, neat stitches.

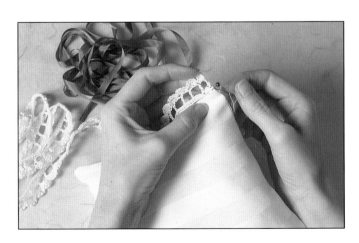

PROJECT 32

Egg Cozies

These egg cozies, crocheted from remnants of brightly colored wool, will certainly cheer up the breakfast table.

YOU WILL NEED
8 ply wool
F/5 crochet hook
a blunt needle
scissors
a tape measure
an egg cup

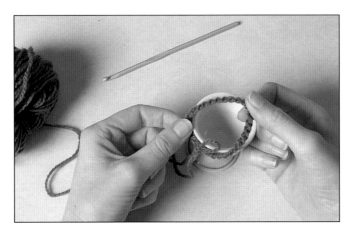

1 ◀ *Measure around the rim of the egg cup. Crochet an even number of chain stitches to a suitable length and sl to form a loop, taking care not to twist.*

2 ▶ *The first row gives a tight holding edge, while the second gives height. In step 3 the cozy takes shape.*
First row: 1 tch, 1 row sc, sl.
Second row: 4 tch, 1 row tr, sl.

*Note: When decreasing (dec), two stitches are crocheted together as follows. Begin the first stitch as usual. Once the hook is inserted into the work, yo and draw back through the work (yo for double) then insert hook into the next stitch along, yo, draw through work, * yo, draw through two loops, repeat from * till only one loop is left on the hook.*

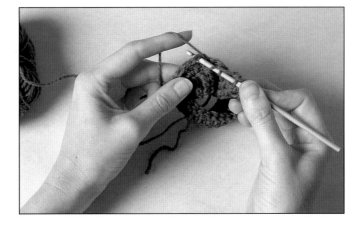

3 ◀ *Rows 3 - 4: * 3 tch, dec 1 at start and end of row, 1 row dc, sl, repeat from *.*
Rows 5 - 7: # 1 tch, dec 1 at start and end of row, 1 row sc, sl, repeat from # for two more rows.
Eighth row: 1 tch, dec all around, 1 row sc, sl.

4 ▶ *Form the cozy's handle as follows:*
10 ch, sl to opposite side, fasten off.
Sew in any loose threads.

PROJECT 33

Baby's Blanket

YOU WILL NEED
8 ply baby wool
D/3 crochet hook
a blunt needle
a tape measure
scissors

Two alternating rows of stitches create a pretty leaf design in this pattern. Make the blanket large enough to wrap baby, such as a yard square.

1 ► Crochet chain in multiples of four to the desired width of the blanket.

2 ► First row: 3 tch, 3 dc, * 2 ch, 2 dc, repeat from * until there are only four stitches left to be crocheted in the row. Finish with 4 dc.

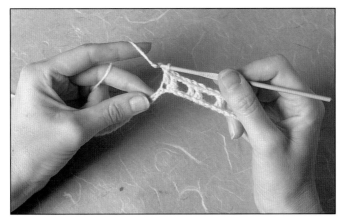

3 ► Second row: 3 tch, 1 dc, * 2 ch, 2 dc, repeat from * to end of row.
When you need to join in a new ball of yarn, simply knot the new yarn to the end of the old one, leaving ends long enough to sew back into the work when finished.

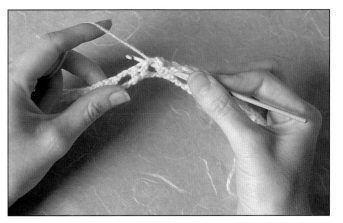

4 ◄ Alternate first and second rows until you have a square: check by folding the blanket diagonally. Fasten off and sew in any loose threads. Press gently.

Suggestion: For added comfort and warmth, you might want to line the blanket and bind the edges.

Needlepoint

Richly woven tapestries were the inspiration for needlepoint or canvaswork, which is why the craft is often referred to as 'tapestry'. Unlike woven works, however, needlepoint is a form of embroidery, worked on a piece of evenly woven mesh or canvas. Like cross-stitch, its stitches are counted. Unlike cross-stitch, needlepoint stitches completely cover the background fabric.

Various stitches, all designed to cover the canvas, can be used on their own, or in combination. Tent stitch, a simple diagonal stitch worked over one cross-band, is often used to fill a whole canvas, mixing different colors into a picture. Pre-printed canvases are generally worked in tent stitch, and you can use it to transfer a pictorial design from a chart onto a blank canvas, as in Project 35. Other stitches, such as the leaf stitch featured in Project 34, can be used to create a pattern rather than a picture.

Needlepoint canvas is referred to by the number of threads per inch; the larger the count, the smaller your stitches will appear. Choose a blunt needle to suit the size of the canvas holes. Several companies make a range of 4-ply wools known as tapestry wool; you can also try working with finer crewel wool, perlé thread, and other types of yarn.

Needlepoint is prone to distortion and it is advisable to use a frame when working. These are rectangular in form, with rollers so you can move your work along a section at a time. Even with a frame, you may find that your work will need to be blocked back into shape before it can be made into anything; see page 13 for details.

Suitable projects for needlepoint are not limitless and you may find that your home fills with cushions if you become an enthusiast! Other possibilities, however, include pictures, chair seats, book covers, and other items which do not need to be particularly flexible.

Canvas comes in different forms and sizes: penelope canvas is woven with a double thread, while mono is a single thread mesh. Plastic canvas is available in limited sizes.

Some very attractive kits, which include a printed canvas and the necessary yarn, can be bought today.

Tent stitch

Scottish stitch, named because of the plaid effect it creates, is actually a combination of tent stitch and larger diagonal stitches, worked in a grid.

This beautiful purse has been worked with fine wool in a bargello pattern, characterized by waves of tonal gradations.

PROJECT 34

Keepsake Box

Make a special box lid using plastic canvas and needlepoint techniques. If you don't have a suitable box base, you can make one from stiff card and strong glue.

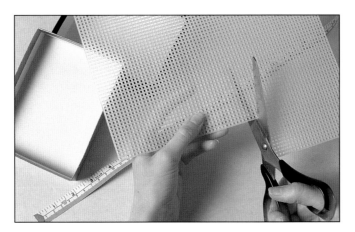

1 ◀ Measure your box base: you will need pieces of plastic canvas slightly larger than the dimensions of the base. Cut canvas pieces for the top and sides, making sure all the edges are trimmed smooth. Select yarn to fit the holes in the canvas.

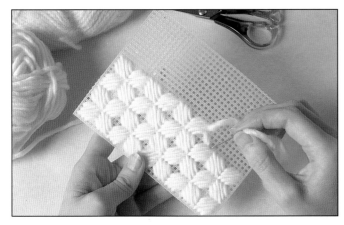

2 ▲ Work the top of the lid in Brighton stitch (see the diagram on this page). Stitch a block of five diagonal stitches, then a second block slanting the other direction, leaving a small unfilled space between them, as shown. Continue, changing the angle each block.

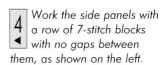

3 ▲ In a contrasting yarn, work an upright cross over the two bars which have been left blank between blocks.

4 ◀ Work the side panels with a row of 7-stitch blocks with no gaps between them, as shown on the left.

5 ▶ Overstitch the side panels and the top together with the contrasting yarn. Join the short edges of the side panels. Overstitch the raw edges of the canvas along the bottom of the side panels for a neat finish.

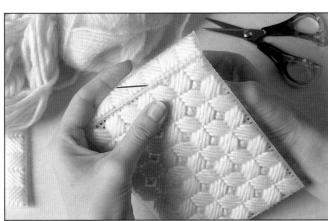

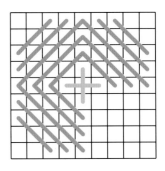

PROJECT 35

Pin Cushion

Tent stitch is a basic unit ideal for building up pictorial images. In this project, it's used to create a charming cherry design.

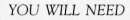

YOU WILL NEED
10-count canvas
tapestry wool
filling material
backing fabric
silk cord
glue
masking tape
a blunt needle
a frame
sewing equipment

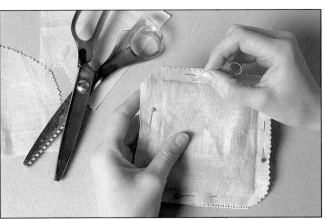

 1 ▲ Bind the edges of the canvas with masking tape and secure it in a frame. Work the design in tent stitch (see page 107), referring to the key for color in the DMC range of tapestry wools.

2 ▲ Trim the canvas ½" from the needlepoint. Cut backing fabric the same size and pin them together, right sides facing. Sew around three sides, stitching very close to the design area.

3 ▶ Trim the corners and turn the work right side out. Fill the cushion with wool or polyester filler and sew the opening closed.

KEY		
Symbol	Color	DMC
•	cream	ecru
■	light red	7107
✕	dark red	7110
+	green	7362
O	dark green	7393
−	light green	7548
U	brown	7845

4 ▼ Cut a length of silken cord and dip the ends in glue to prevent fraying. Sew it around the cushion, concealing the seam.

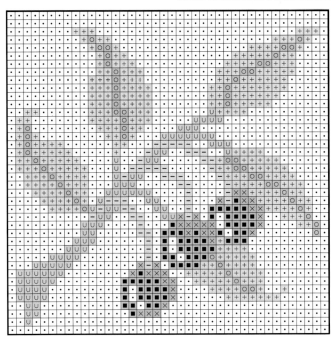

PROJECT 36

Doorstop

A leaf pattern turns a very ordinary brick into an attractive doorstop. This one is worked with soft embroidery cotton, but you could substitute hard-wearing wool.

YOU WILL NEED
10-count canvas
yarns
a brick
felt
lining fabric
a marker
a blunt needle
a frame
sewing equipment

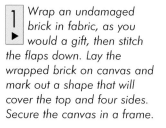

1 Wrap an undamaged brick in fabric, as you would a gift, then stitch the flaps down. Lay the wrapped brick on canvas and mark out a shape that will cover the top and four sides. Secure the canvas in a frame.

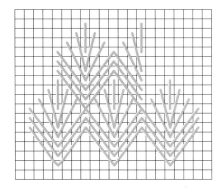

2 Working within the marked area of the canvas, stitch the leaf design in horizontal rows. Begin at the bottom left-hand corner of each leaf and stitch the first half, then the second half. Note the hole under the top stitch. When each row is complete, work the row directly above. Continue until the marked area is complete.

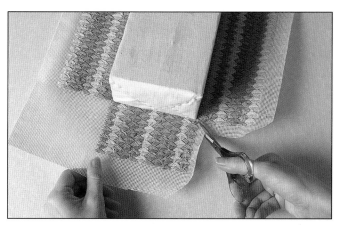

3 Remove the work from the frame and block it if it is distorted. Check that the work is the right size before trimming the canvas around the needlepoint. Fold the bare flaps in and use a strong thread to overstitch the sides together.

4 Lace the bottom flaps together. Cut a rectangle of felt for the base and stitch it onto the canvas with a matching thread.

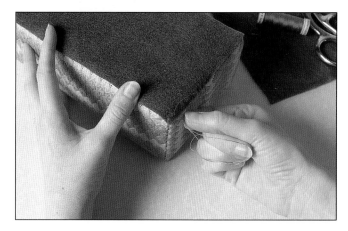

Cross-stitch

Cross-stitch is one of the most popular crafts and, as such, deserves a chapter of its own. The basic stitch is very easy to learn and yet can be used as a unit in quite complex designs. Its potential has long been recognized; the first examples of cross-stitch were found in ancient times when it was used to piece animal skins together. In the sixteenth century, cross-stitch was mostly worked by court ladies and so was a sign of status. Today, the range of fabrics, threads and the wealth of designs available means anyone can create heirlooms to treasure.

Cross-stitch is one form of counted embroidery; a charted pattern is transferred onto a piece of evenly woven, unmarked fabric by counting threads or bands of threads. The charted pattern is a grid of squares with symbols (or blocks of color) forming the design.

A key accompanying each pattern tells you which color of embroidery thread relates to which symbol. Working the design is simply a matter of stitching a series of crosses in the appropriate thread color according to the arrangement on the chart.

The most popular of evenweave fabrics is Aida cloth, which is available in a wide range of colors. Aida is formed with bands of threads and is described by the number of bands per inch, so 14-count Aida will have 14 bands (and stitches) to the inch. Linen is measured by the number of threads per inch but each stitch is worked over two threads, so on a 22-count linen, you would work 11 stitches per inch.

Choose a blunt needle, such as a small tapestry needle, that will not split the fabric threads. Match the size of the needle to the size of the fabric hole.

The top two fabrics are Aida cloth; the bottom one is an evenweave linen.

Stranded cottons, which can be divided to suit the fabric count, are ideal for cross-stitch.

Working with an embroidery hoop
will help prevent warping and
reduce handling of the fabric when
you are stitching large designs.

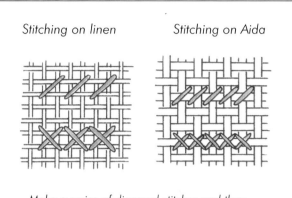

Stitching on linen   *Stitching on Aida*

Make a series of diagonal stitches and then
return along the row, making a second
series of diagonal stitches to form crosses.
Start and tail ends are secured under stitches
at the back.

The simplicity of cross-stitch
makes it ideal for children to
learn as an introduction to
embroidery. Give them a small
project, such as finger puppets
or the letter of their name.

PROJECT 37

Guest Towel

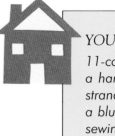

YOU WILL NEED
11-count Aida fabric
a handtowel
stranded cotton
a blunt needle
sewing equipment

A repeat, one-color design is a good beginning for anyone new to cross-stitch. This classical border design makes a stylish trim for a guest towel.

1 ▶ Cut a strip of 11-count Aida fabric, 2 " wide and 2 " longer than the width of your handtowel. Thread a blunt needle with two strands of embroidery cotton (DMC 798 is used here) and start stitching the design at one end of the Aida strip. A diagram on page 115 shows how to cross-stitch.

2 ▶ Repeat the pattern as many times as necessary, working the end bars of the design only at the start and finish of the strip. Fold and press a hem along all edges of the Aida strip to fit the towel.

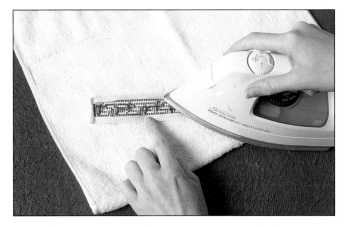

3 ▶ Pin the strip onto the towel and then sew it neatly in place, with a row of stitches one square in from the edges.

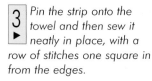

PROJECT 38

Birth Sampler

A sampler is a lovely way to commemorate a child's birth.
Rearrange the letters and numbers to form a name and
birth date which personalize the work.

YOU WILL NEED
14-count Aida fabric
stranded cotton
a blunt needle
strong thread
stiff cardboard
a knife & mat
a ruler
a frame

1 Cut a piece of 14-count Aida fabric, 15 x 14 ". Prevent fraying by staystitching the edges or applying masking tape. Fold the fabric in half and mark the fold with basting stitches. Fold the fabric the other way and mark this line in the same way to indicate the center of the fabric.

2 Start stitching an area near the marked center of the pattern, which appears on page 159. The key below identifies thread colors corresponding to each charted symbol. Thread a blunt needle with two strands of embroidery cotton. A diagram on page 115 shows how to cross-stitch.

	KEY	
Symbol	Color	DMC
+	mauve	211
×	peach	352
U	tan	402
–	yellow	744
*	blue	794
O	green	3348

3 When all stitching is complete, remove the basting stitches. Hand-wash the work if necessary and press gently, with the embroidery face down on a folded towel.

4 Cut a rectangle of cardboard larger than the design to suit your frame. Position the card over the work so that it is centered. Using a strong thread, make long lacing stitches from top to bottom and then side to side so that the work is stretched evenly over the cardboard. Frame the sampler.

PROJECT 39

Needle Case

This medieval motif, stitched in jewel-like colors on red Aida cloth, makes a stunning adornment for a needle case.

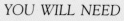

1 Cut a 9½ x 5½ " piece of red 14-count Aida. Tape the edges with masking tape. Stitch the design on one half of the fabric, 1¼ " in from the edge, as shown.

2 Cut two 3½ " squares of thin cardboard. Fold the fabric in half and position one card on one side of the crease. Fold the edges of the fabric over. Using strong thread, make long lacing stitches to secure the card. Secure the other card on the other half.

3 Cut two or three 3 x 6½ " pieces of thin blue felt. Sew the felt layers together with a few long stitches down the 'centerfold' of the felt pages.

	KEY	
Symbol	Color	DMC
−	blue	798
O	green	3819
✕	gold	3820

4 Lay the felt pages on the inside of the card casing and handsew the bottom page onto the Aida fabric with small overcasting stitches.

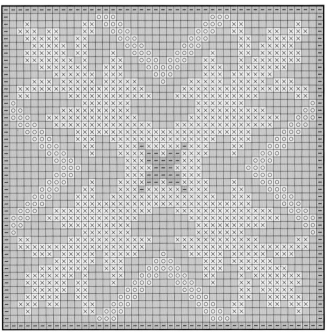

Embroidery

The craft of decorating fabric with stitchery is very nearly as old and widespread a practice as the use of fabric itself. Throughout the centuries and across the world, dozens of stitches have been developed, each with a different decorative potential. Some, such as satin stitch, are very flexible units; others, such as cretan stitch, are more pronounced in their effect. The stitches used in projects in this book are shown on the next page.

Embroidery can generally be divided into two types. In counted thread work, the weave of the ground fabric determines the size and arrangement of the stitches. In surface embroidery, the stitcher has more latitude and stitch size and direction is determined more by the shape of the motif to be worked.

Blackwork is in some ways a combination of both types: regular composite-stitches are repeated to fill the outline of an irregular motif. In well-designed blackwork, the density of the stitches is used to suggest tonal differences in the design. Candlewicking, of which the pin cushion below is an example, is another form of mono-color work, in which the stitch texture is all important.

EMBROIDERY STITCHES

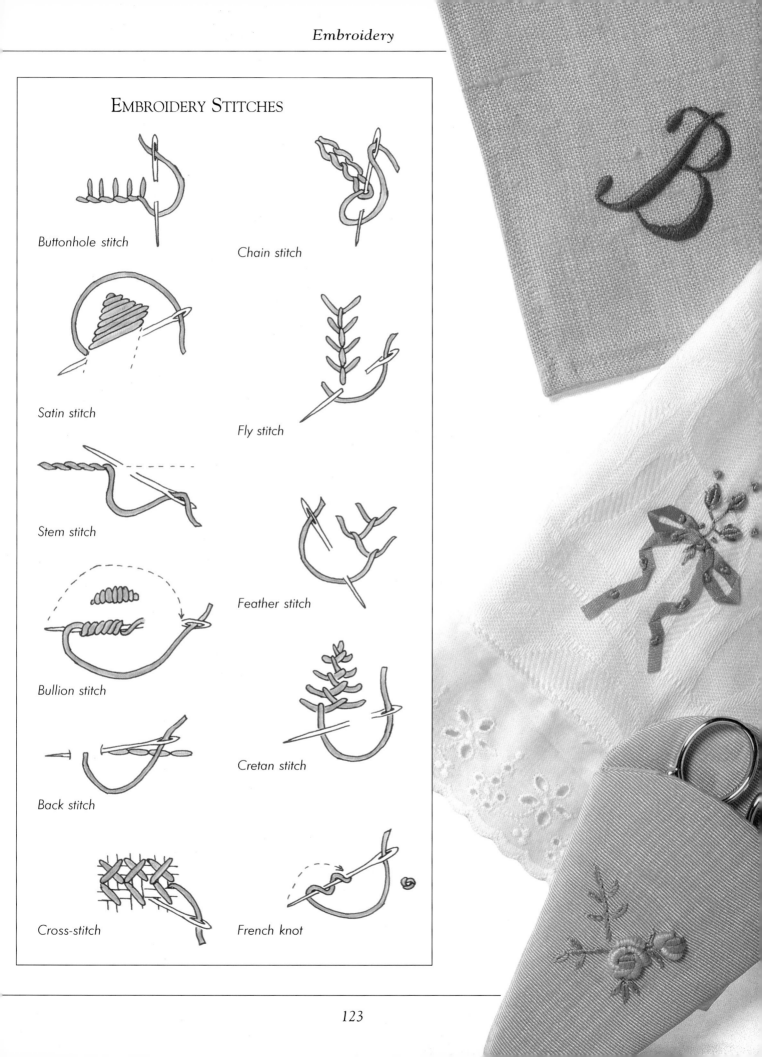

Buttonhole stitch

Chain stitch

Satin stitch

Fly stitch

Stem stitch

Feather stitch

Bullion stitch

Back stitch

Cretan stitch

Cross-stitch

French knot

PROJECT 40

Bookmark

Satin stitch strikes a charming note on this bookmark, ideal as a gift for anyone who has an ear (and an eye) for music!

1 Cut an 11 x 6 " piece of lightweight fabric. Trace the design in dark pen. Tape the fabric over the tracing and transfer the design onto the fabric.

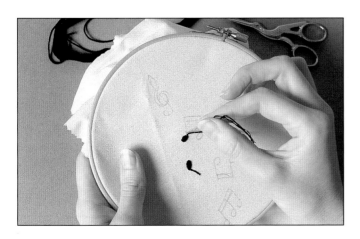

2 Stitch the design using 3 strands of black stranded cotton. The lines are worked in stem stitch and the solid areas in satin stitch. See page 123 for stitch instructions. When complete, press the work lightly.

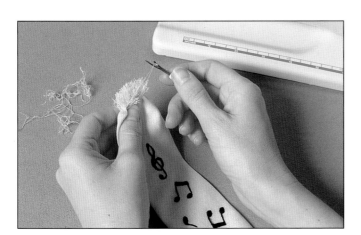

3 Fold the fabric in half with the two long edges together and sew a 1 " seam. Turn the bookmark right side out and press flat with the seam in the center. Tease out threads at each end of the bookmark to create a fringe. If the fabric frays easily, overcast the fringed edges to secure.

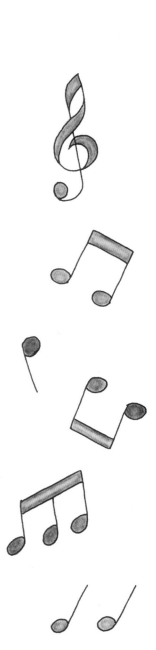

PROJECT 41

Candlewick Bag

The appeal of candlewick embroidery lies in the textural patterns created. Here a heart of satin stitch, French knots and back stitch decorates an heirloom bag.

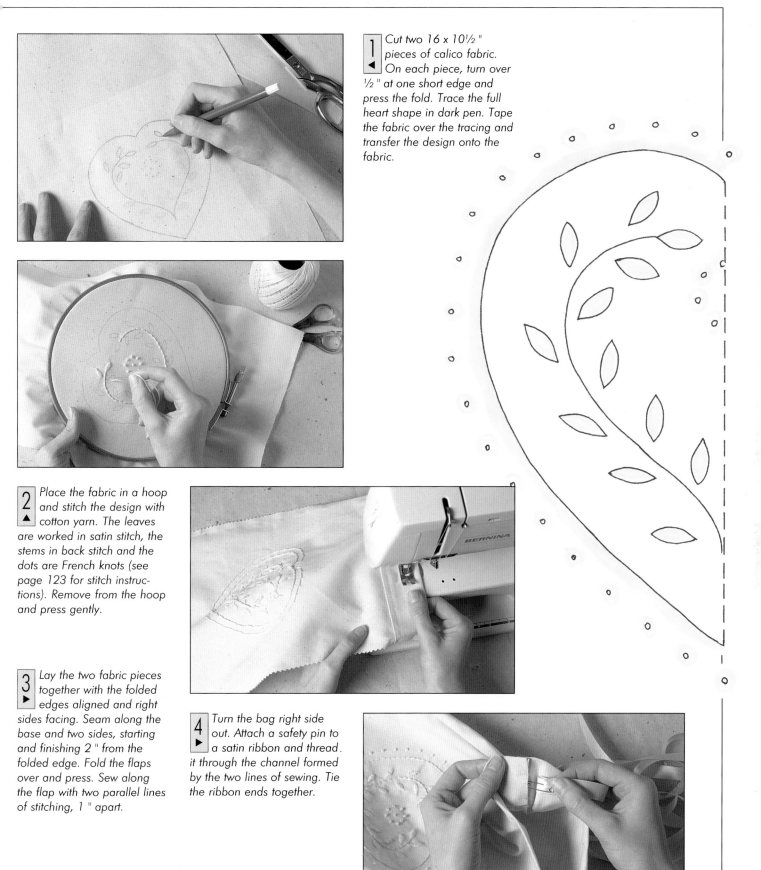

1 Cut two 16 x 10½ " pieces of calico fabric. On each piece, turn over ½ " at one short edge and press the fold. Trace the full heart shape in dark pen. Tape the fabric over the tracing and transfer the design onto the fabric.

2 Place the fabric in a hoop and stitch the design with cotton yarn. The leaves are worked in satin stitch, the stems in back stitch and the dots are French knots (see page 123 for stitch instructions). Remove from the hoop and press gently.

3 Lay the two fabric pieces together with the folded edges aligned and right sides facing. Seam along the base and two sides, starting and finishing 2 " from the folded edge. Fold the flaps over and press. Sew along the flap with two parallel lines of stitching, 1 " apart.

4 Turn the bag right side out. Attach a safety pin to a satin ribbon and thread it through the channel formed by the two lines of sewing. Tie the ribbon ends together.

PROJECT 42

Tray Cloth

YOU WILL NEED
evenweave linen
stranded cotton
bias binding
a blunt needle
sewing equipment

Blackwork stitches are traditionally used to fill pictorial designs. Here, however, is a 'sampler' to introduce this attractive form of needlework.

1 ◀ Cut a piece of even-weave linen to fit your tray. Fold and hem along the top and bottom edges. Pin black bias binding along the side edges and sew it in place with small stitches in black sewing thread so that it binds the raw edges.

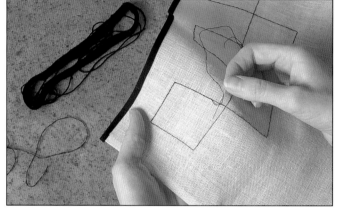

2 ▲ The design squares must contain an even number of threads across and down. Mark them out using a strand of black stranded cotton with whipped back stitch. This is worked by back stitching and then whipping another thread over each back stitch without entering the fabric.

3 ▼ Fill in each square with a different pattern by following the picture on the right. Use one strand of black stranded cotton. Most stitches are worked over two threads of the fabric.

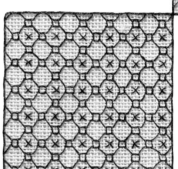

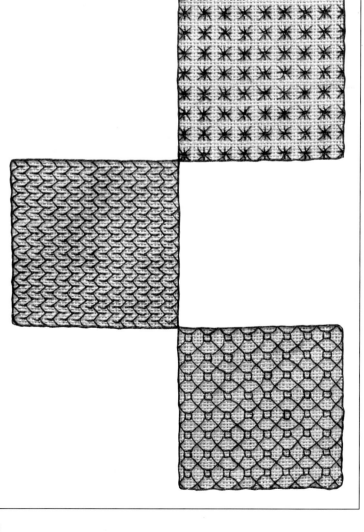

Machine Embroidery

Although sewing machines were originally invented for practical and commercial purposes, one of the side benefits has been their use as an extra tool for embroidery. The effects achieved with machine embroidery are entirely different to those achieved by hand and it is possibly a less soothing form of craftwork, but there is plenty of scope for individual creativity and experimentation.

You don't need the latest model of sewing machine; a basic domestic model will do. To begin with, experiment with your machine until you have explored all its possibilities and the effects that can be achieved with different threads and fabrics. To be successful at machine embroidery, you must know what your machine will and won't do.

There are two types of machine embroidery: automatic and free. The first depends on the potential of the machine; all you have to do is set it and guide the fabric through. Recent models can even be programmed by computer to plot and produce whole designs. With free machine embroidery, you simply use the two most basic stitches – straight and zigzag – and the results depend on your skill and imagination. Stitch at the slowest possible speed, giving you maximum control.

One limitation is that you can only use threads suitable for a sewing machine; some threads are made specifically for machine embroidery work. Most fabrics can be used, with the exception of stretchy knits. The best fabrics for first attempts are medium to heavy weights. Later, try other materials like silk, satin, rayon, paper, organza, velvet, or indeed anything that the needle will pass through!

A small hoop holds the fabric taut. Fix the fabric in the hoop so it sits on the bed of the machine.

Machine embroidery requires less handling of the material, so paper can be used in place of fabric. This opens up possibilities for paper collage and combining paint and thread in a very artistic way.

▲ When using the sewing machine normally, the feed dog – two rows of teeth under the needle – move the fabric along at a regular pace, producing even stitches. When this is lowered or removed (check your machine's manual) the stitch size is determined by the way you move the fabric.

The pressure foot should also be removed, although you may find it helpful to replace it with a darning foot which will prevent puckering. Remember to lower the pressure bar, which creates top tension, or the thread will tangle underneath.

Zigzag can be very decorative and is a good starting point. The even zigzag stitches around the frame below were sewn with the feed dog raised.

This perfect motif was created on a programmable sewing machine.

PROJECT 43

Eye Pillow

Filled with lightweight linseed and lavender, an eye pillow can be very soothing when laid over resting eyes. An embroidered one makes a thoughful gift.

YOU WILL NEED
satin
organza
gold thread
tissue paper
a pencil
linseed
lavender
a sewing machine
sewing equipment

1 Trace the pattern onto tissue paper. Cut a 7 " square of satin and a matching one of organza. Lay the organza on the satin and pin the tracing on one side. Place the work in a small embroidery hoop.

2 Work with gold thread suitable for use in a sewing machine. Lower or remove the machine's feed dog and stitch along the design lines, moving the hoop as you work. Tie off thread ends at the back. Gently tear away the tissue paper.

3 On one of the pillows shown, the organza has been carefully trimmed close to the stitching with a pair of curved scissors.

4 Fold the work in half with right sides facing and sew a ½ " seam along two sides, leaving a gap for turning. Turn the pillow right side out. Spoon in linseed (or another grain) with dried lavender until it is three-quarters full. Handsew the opening closed.

PROJECT 44

Stitched Frame

Machine embroidery can be worked on thick paper to outline and define painted designs, as in this floral picture frame.

YOU WILL NEED
watercolor paper
watercolors
a brush
cardboard
glue
a knife & cutting mat
tracing paper
a pencil & ruler
machine threads
a sewing machine

1 Measure your photograph. Cut a piece of thick watercolor paper with a window slightly smaller than the photo and a border 2" wide. Cut cardboard to the same size but without the window. Trace the stand pattern onto card and cut along the solid lines with a knife.

2 Paint a design onto the paper frame in colors to suit your picture. Watercolor pencils are particularly easy to use: you simply draw with the pencils and then wash over the work with a wet brush. Allow the paint to dry.

3 Lower or remove the machine's feed dog and straight stitch around the design in a darker color to add detail. Move the paper as you work but keep your hands well clear of the needle. Tie off thread ends at the back.

4 Assemble the picture frame as follows. Position the photo behind the frame and glue or tape it in place. Glue on the backing section. Run a knife over the dashed lines on the stand and bend it into shape. Glue the stand onto the backing to suit the orientation of your photograph.

PROJECT 45

Valentine Cards

A sewing machine can help you quickly fill in areas of a design, such as these love-struck hearts. You could also try motifs for other occasions.

YOU WILL NEED
base fabric
card
a marker
a knife & cutting mat
a ruler
double-sided tape
machine threads
a sewing machine

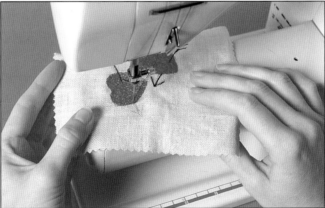

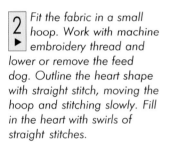

1 ▲ Sketch the pattern on fabric with a marker pen or tailor's chalk. If the fabric is light, you may be able to trace over the design.

2 ▶ Fit the fabric in a small hoop. Work with machine embroidery thread and lower or remove the feed dog. Outline the heart shape with straight stitch, moving the hoop and stitching slowly. Fill in the heart with swirls of straight stitches.

3 ◀ Remove the embroidery from the hoop and stitch the arrows. Tie off thread ends at the back.

4 ◀ Cut card 18 x 6 " and cut a 3½ " square window in the center. Fold the card into thirds and trim a narrow strip off one end. Machine around the window with zigzag stitch. Trim the embroidery and mount it in the window, using double-sided tape to hold it in place and to stick down the trimmed back flap.

Wool Embroidery

Embroidering on and with wool is quite different to working with other materials. The soft sheen and fine nature of embroidery threads are sacrificed for a much coarser effect. The advantages, however, are that a decorative effect can be achieved with wool more quickly and a range of new items can be embellished.

Crewel work is embroidery stitched, as you might expect, in crewel woolen yarn. It was especially popular amongst the Jacobeans of seventeenth century Britain who lived at a time when printed fabrics were scarce. To decorate furnishings and other items for which fine needlework would have been too time consuming, they developed a style of embroidering with wool. Though the work was intricate, the motifs and stitches tended to be large in scale. Crewel work often represented floral motifs in an idealized and rather unrealistic way and the style was heavily influenced by the Eastern cultures with whom the Jacobeans were trading.

The modern descendent of crewel work is a simplified version, still with flowers as the main preoccupation. We now tend to reserve wool for working on woolen blanketing and the coarse nature of this fabric tends to exaggerate the coarseness of the embroidery. It is however, ideal for making warm items: baby's blankets, dressing gowns, covers for hot water bottles, and so on. It is also a lovely fabric for soft toys, as in Project 48.

Brightly colored yarns could also be used to decorate a pair of plain woolen gloves. When decorating knitted fabrics made with a relatively large stitch, you can choose from surface embroidery, where the stitches are relatively unconstrained, or counted work, either in cross-stitch or duplicate stitch, as in Project 28.

1 Pompoms are fun to make from remnants of wool. Mark two circles on a piece of cardboard and then mark a smaller circle inside each one. Cut these out to give you two matching cardboard rings. Thread a blunt needle with wool and, holding the rings together, wrap the wool around them.

2 Continue wrapping until the cardboard rings are covered and the hole is filled. Insert the blades of embroidery scissors between the rings and cut the wool right around.

3 Ease the cardboard rings apart and bind the strands with a short length of yarn. Knot this and trim the ends, or leave them as a means of securing the pompom onto a project. Remove the cardboard rings and trim the pompom neatly.

Crewel wool or Persian wool (which is three strands of crewel wool loosely twisted together) will give a finer effect than the thicker tapestry wool.

PROJECT 46

Beret

YOU WILL NEED
a woolen beret
tapestry wool
adhesive paper
a pencil
a large blunt needle
sewing equipment

*Turn a plain woolen beret into a work of art
with sprays of flowers, worked in a few stitches
with scraps of tapestry wool.*

1 ▶ Cut circles of adhesive paper, roughly the size of the desired flowers. Arrange these in groups of three or four around the beret to indicate where to stitch.

2 ▶ Thread a large blunt needle with tapestry wool. Work lazy daisy stitch as shown, forming a loop of wool the right size and then securing it with a small stitch. Stitch five petals for each flower, stitching each petal opposite the last, rather than working around the flower.

3 ▶ In a contrasting color, stitch a French knot at the center of each flower. See page 123 for a diagram showing how to work this stitch.

4 ▶ With green tapestry wool, embroider leaves with pairs of straight stitches. Complete all the flowers around the beret, removing the adhesive markers as you work each one.

PROJECT 47

Hot Bottle Bag

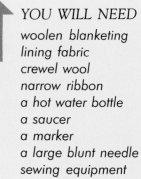

YOU WILL NEED
woolen blanketing
lining fabric
crewel wool
narrow ribbon
a hot water bottle
a saucer
a marker
a large blunt needle
sewing equipment

*Here's a pretty way to keep snug during the winter months.
The measurements given fit an 8"-wide bottle; adjust them
for a different size.*

1 ▶ Cut two pieces of woolen blanketing, each 16 x 11 ". Using a saucer approximately 5 " in diameter, round two corners of each piece and mark a circle on the top section with a water-soluble marker.

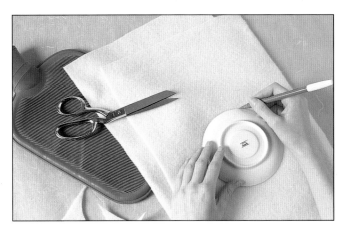

2 ▶ Refer to the pattern on page 156 and mark the main roses around your circle. Roses are worked as follows: 4 parallel straight stitches in dark pink, then 4 sets of 3 diagonal stitches in lighter pink as in the diagram. The leaves are fly stitches (see page 123). The rosebuds are 3 pink stitches plus a green fly stitch. The stems are back stitch.

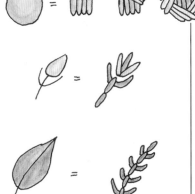

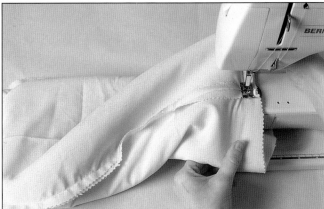

3 ◀ Sew the woolen sections together, right sides facing, leaving the opening unsewn. Cut two pieces of lining fabric and make a matching bag. Turn the embroidered bag right side out and insert the lining bag. Turn the opening of both bags in and handsew the lining to the bag.

4 ▶ Thread a large needle with a length of narrow ribbon. 2 " down from the opening of the bag, make a series of long stitches through both the wool and the lining, starting and ending at the front center. Insert the bottle, draw in the neck and tie a bow.

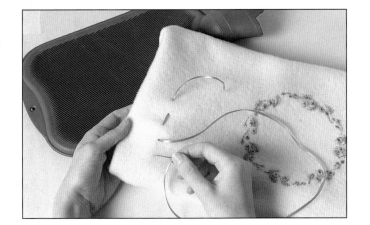

PROJECT 48

Easter Bunny

Woolen blanketing is an ideal material for making soft toys. This vivacious rabbit will charm the young at Easter or, indeed, at any time of the year.

YOU WILL NEED

woolen blanketing
perlé thread
stranded cotton
wool
narrow ribbon
polyester filler
tracing paper
a marker
a large blunt needle
sewing equipment

1 ▶ Trace the rabbit pattern on page 158 onto paper (note that only half the design is given). On woolen blanketing, mark out two body sections and four ear sections, each with a seam allowance all around. Cut out the pieces.

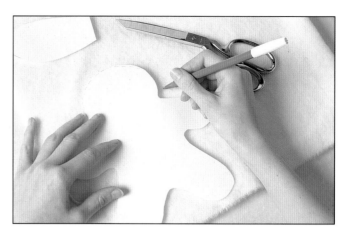

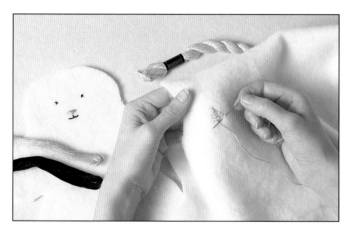

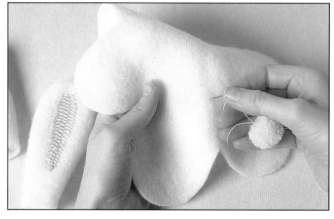

2 ▲ Stitch the face with stranded cotton: cross-stitch eyes, a satin stitch nose and a back stitch mouth. On two ear sections, work a series of cretan stitches in perlé thread. See page 123 for stitch details.

3 ▲ Lay the two sections for one ear together, right sides facing, and seam around the curved edge. Turn. Sew the other ear the same way. Make a pompom with white wool (see page 139) and stitch it on the back section as a tail.

4 ▶ Lay the two sections of the body together, right sides facing, with the ears positioned as shown. Seam around the edges, leaving a gap for turning. Trim the edges and snip darts at sharp curves. Turn the toy right side out.

5 ◀ Fill the toy evenly with polyester filler and handstitch the opening closed. Make a small bow with narrow ribbon and stitch it on at the rabbit's neck.

Gold & Silver

Metallic threadwork, especially gold and silver, is the richest type of embroidery, both in appearance and cost. Throughout history, this form of embroidery has maintained an exceptionally high standard of design and craftsmanship, presumably because the materials were so expensive.

Textiles embroidered in gold are referred to in Greek literature and writers have made mention of such adornments ever since. In the fourteenth century, silver-gilt work was embroidered by professionals who were given commissions by churches for vestments, altar cloths and banners. By the sixteenth century, gold and silver threads were used in elaborate designs on the costumes of courtiers. Over the next two centuries, metallic work took on an Eastern look, due to the influence of imports from India and China. The nineteenth century saw a loss of interest in metallic embroidery, a decline we are only just starting to come out of.

The beauty of metal thread work lies in the textures and the way light plays on, and is reflected by, the varied surfaces of the threads and cords. Many of the colors sold, especially the golds, are quite garish and it is worthwhile hunting for more subtle tones.

Metallic threads come in many forms. Japanese gold threads are made from gold leaf wrapped around a silk core. Tambour is a fine metal thread suitable for stitching. Fine metal threads can also be hand-twisted into cords; see the instructions on page 15. Synthetic threads, such as lurex, may be used for stitching and can be washed.

Stranded metal threads can be separated into finer strands.

Today, you can even buy
metallic threads suitable for
use in a sewing machine,
making it a simple matter to
add a touch of pomp to plain
fabrics.

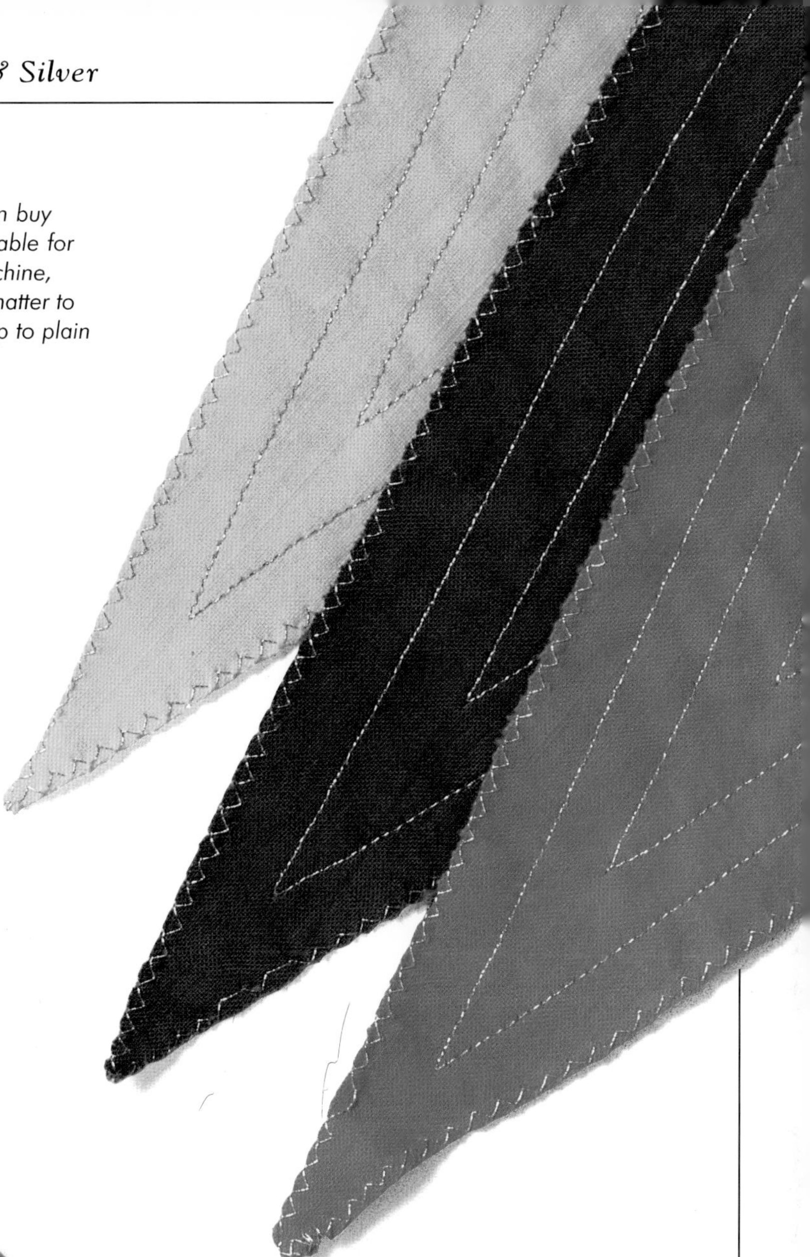

Metallic threads are
now available in a
wide range of hues,
including gradated
and multicolors.

Couching

Threads which lack flexibility or
cannot easily be drawn through the
ground fabric can be couched, that is,
arranged on top of the fabric and
secured with tiny stitches in a finer
thread. It is an ideal method for
working curves and spirals quickly
and has the added advantage that no
valuable thread is wasted at the back
where it won't be seen.

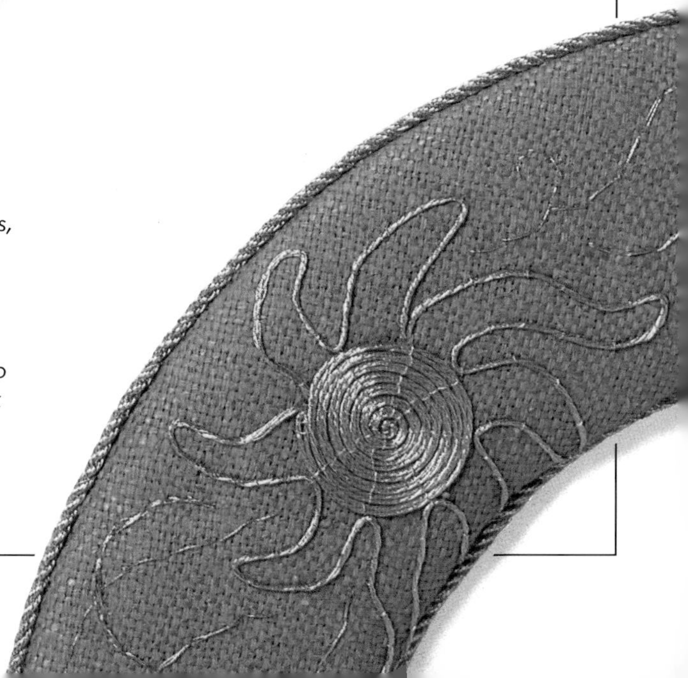

PROJECT 49

Tooth Fairy Bag

YOU WILL NEED
blue velvet
gold lining fabric
stranded gold thread
an unpicker
a sewing machine
sewing equipment

Here's an enchanted bag for keeping that tooth safe until the tooth fairy visits. The stars are worked with, appropriately, 'star filling stitch'.

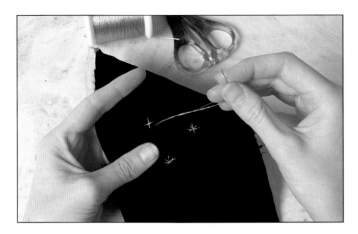

1 Cut an 11 x 4½ " piece of blue velvet and staystitch the edges. Stitch gold thread as follows: first stitch an upright cross, then work a diagonal cross on top and complete it with a tiny cross which secures the stitch as shown. Work as many stars as you like.

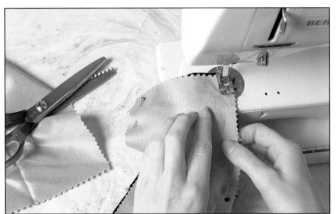

2 Cut gold fabric to the same size as the velvet. Lay the two together, right sides facing, and seam along the two long edges and one short edge. Turn the work right side out, turn the raw edges in and handsew the last seam. You should now have a lined rectangle.

3 1 " down from one short edge, sew three button-holes, evenly spaced. 1 " down from the opposite short edge, sew four buttonholes. Lay a pin along the top and use an unpicker to cut each buttonhole open.

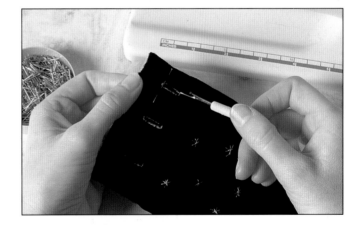

4 Fold the rectangle so the lining is concealed and handsew the sides of the bag neatly. Cut three 20 " lengths of gold thread and braid them to form a cord. Knot each end. Lace the cord through the buttonholes and knot the ends together.

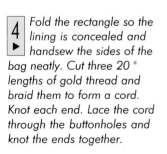

PROJECT 50

Paperweight

Using small couching stitches, thick gold cord is fixed in a Celtic knot. This stylish paperweight would make a useful gift.

1 Trace the knot pattern. Measure the recess of the paperweight and resize the pattern if necessary.

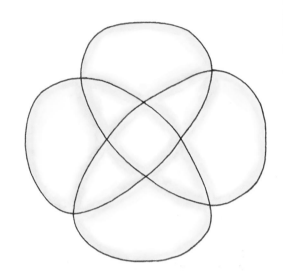

2 Arrange the cord in the pattern. Trim and bind the ends tightly with fine gold thread. Make sure the join is concealed under another section of the pattern.

3 Thread a needle with fine gold thread and secure one end in the felt. Couch the cord in place with a series of slanting stitches in the direction of the twisted cord, picking up the felt under the cord.

4 Cut the felt to fit the recess. Insert it in the paperweight and seal it in place with the cover provided.

PROJECT 51

Mirror Frame

This frame, decorated with stranded metallic threads, will always give you a celestial view of the world. The dimensions given fit a 5½ " mirror.

YOU WILL NEED
fabric
gold & silver thread
a round mirror
wadding
thick card
a compass
a marker
a knife & cutting mat
glue
tape

1 From thick card, cut three disks, each with a 9½ " diameter. From the first, cut out a circle with a diameter of 5¾ "; this ring forms the front of the frame. From the second disk, remove a circle 5½ " in diameter; this ring houses the mirror. The third disk is the backing.

2 Cut a 12 " square of fabric. With water-soluble pen or chalk, trace the outlines of the front ring. Mark a circular sun and a crescent moon.

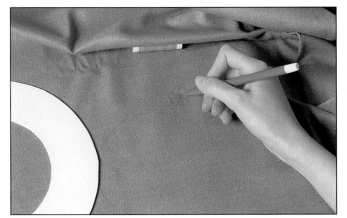

3 Divide the sun circle into eight segments. Cut a long gold thread and fold it in half. Secure this doubled thread at the edge of the circle with a fine couching thread, as shown. Coil the doubled thread around the circle, securing it with a couching stitch at each spoke and working inwards. Secure all ends at the back.

4 Couch the moon in the same way as the sun, but bending the silver thread to form a crescent. Back stitch a series of curved and wavy lines around the ring, using finer gold and silver threads.

5 Glue the front ring onto wadding, then trim it. Lay this onto the back of the embroidery. Cut darts around the ring and tape the fabric tabs on the back of the ring. Cut and tape the center likewise. Couch gold cord around the inside and outside rims. Assemble the frame sections and secure with glue.

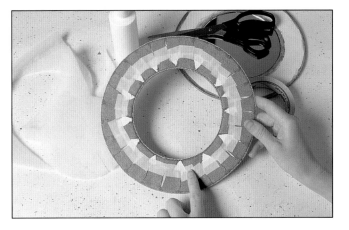

Gift Giving

Needlecrafts are so varied and so full of possibilities that you should never be at a loss for a gift idea again! Many of the projects in this book make wonderful and practical gifts and it is always a pleasure to receive something which has been handmade.

Some of the techniques in this book can also be used to add to the presentation of the gift.

Hand-twisted cords and simple tassels can add a very decorative touch to a plain wrapping or a simple box. For special presents, you could embroider a small motif on a fabric gift bag or sachet.

A greeting card decorated with embroidery will be very welcome. To frame a piece of fabric in a card, use a three-panel mount such as those shown on the opposite page. Blank mounts can be bought in craft stores or you can make your own by folding a piece of cardboard into three panels, cutting a window in the center panel, and securing the fabric behind it.

To make cards speedily, try some machine embroidery directly onto strong paper or thin cardboard. Combining this method with appliqué techniques could produce something quite innovative and unusual.

A few hand-rolled
ribbon roses add
a special touch to
a small gift.

Cross-stitch can be
worked quite quickly
into simple but
eloquent motifs.

This tulip design has
been embroidered
in satin stitch, using
stranded cotton on
linen fabric.

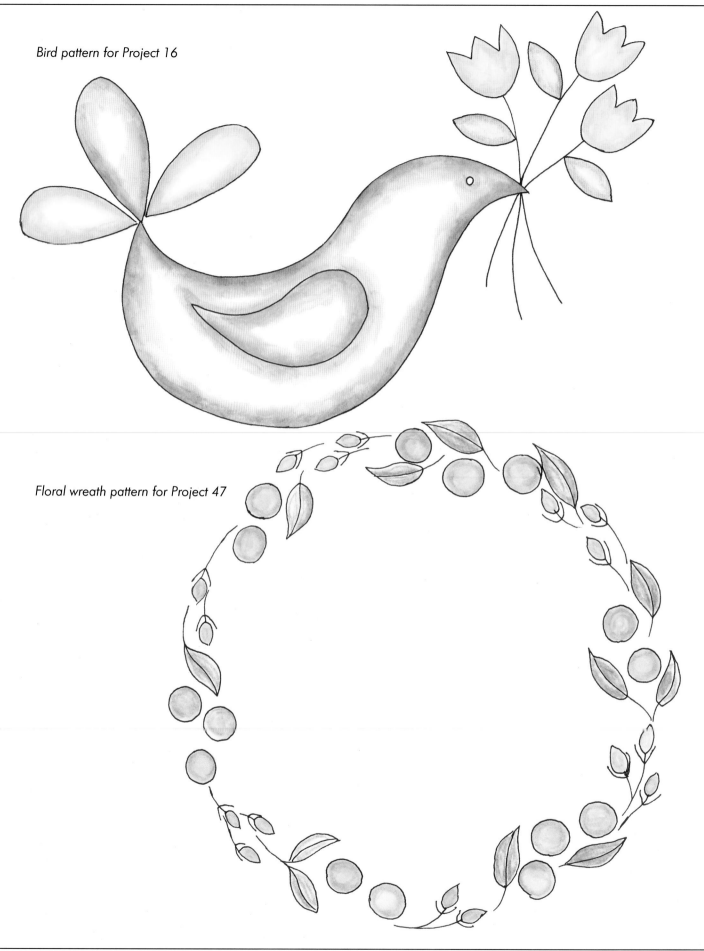

Bird pattern for Project 16

Floral wreath pattern for Project 47

Apron pattern for Project 17

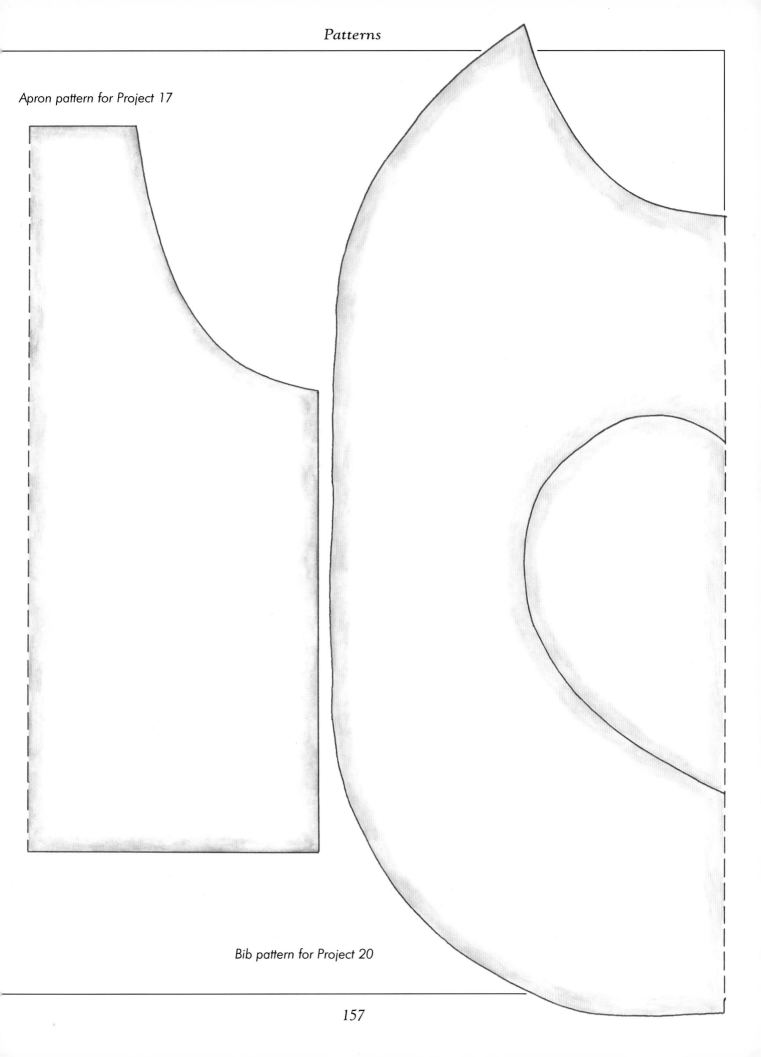

Bib pattern for Project 20

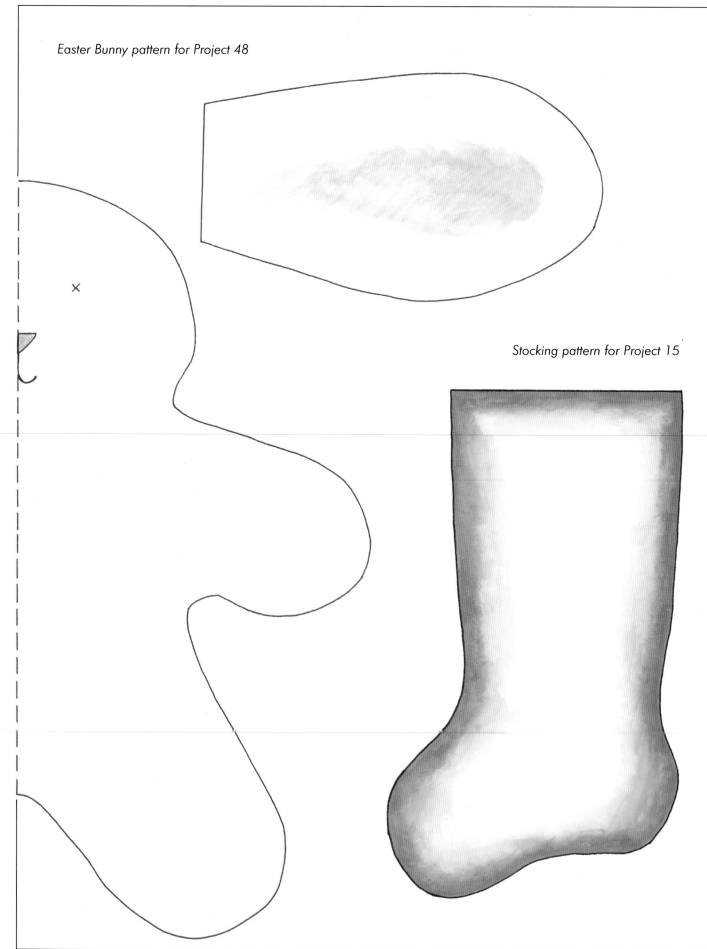

Easter Bunny pattern for Project 48

Stocking pattern for Project 15

Sampler chart for Project 38

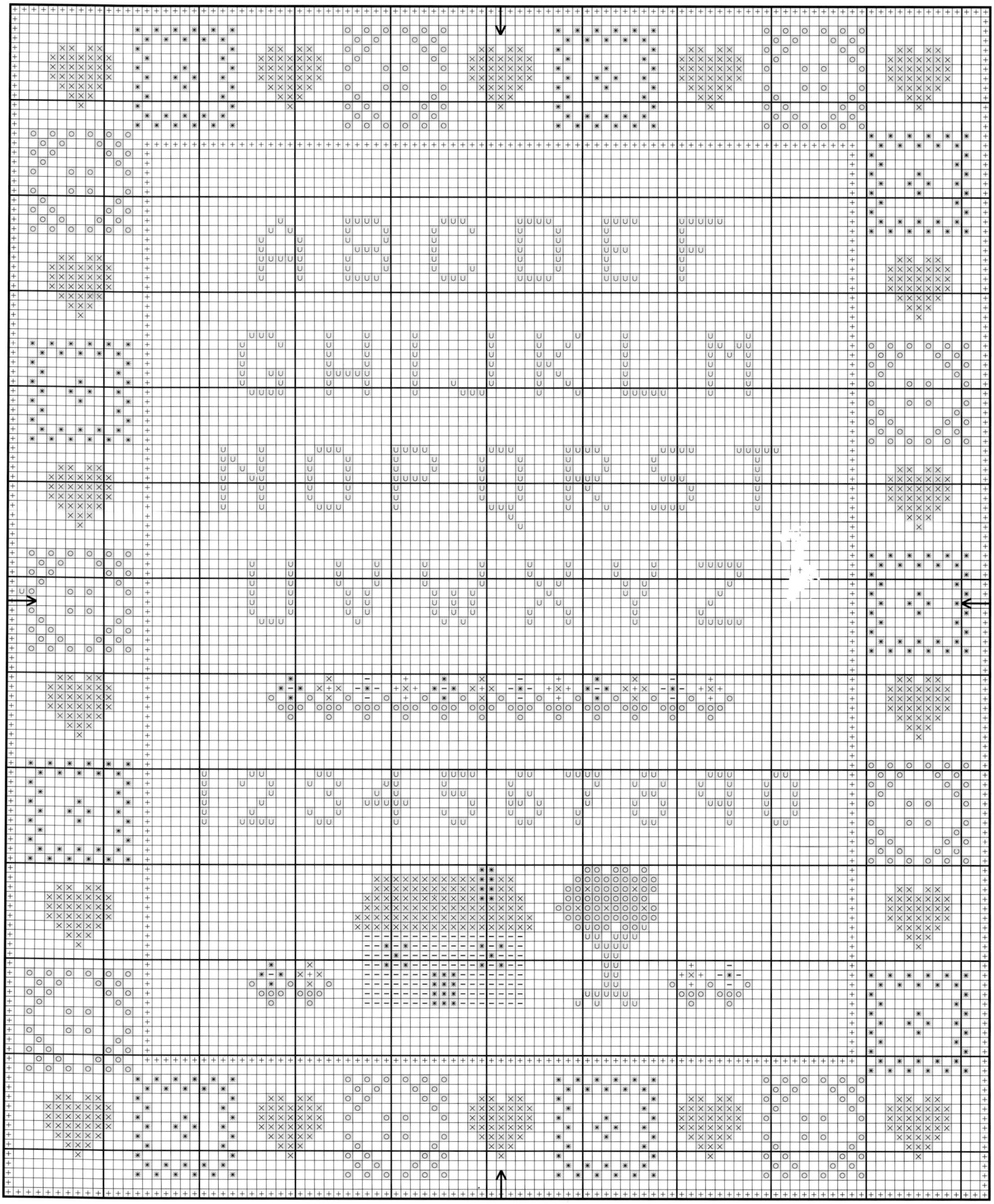

Index

Acknowledgments & Sources

The publisher would like to thank the following for materials and items which appear in this book:

Leonie Draper - for the crochet projects.

Betty Marsh & Shirley Souter - for their help in making various projects in the book.

Lillian Stammer - for the purse on page 39.

Craft With Class - for the guest towel on page 123, the machined motif on page 131, and the wool embroidery on page 138. These and other items are available from the Rocks Market in Sydney.

Charts were created on *Stitchcraft*, Windows-based software. For information, contact Crafted Software (Australia) on Tel: 61 47 573136 Fax: 61 47 573337 or Stitchdesign (USA) at Tel/Fax: 1 (801) 269-1948.